Clean Eating Cookbook Box Set

Clean Eating Cookbook Box Set: Clean Eating Breakfast, Lunch, Dinner & Smoothie Recipes

By Charity Wilson

Table of Contents

Introduction

Thank you for purchasing **"Clean Eating Cookbook Box Set."** I hope you find some new and exciting additions to your collection of clean eating recipes. Here is what you have to look forward to:

Clean Eating Cookbook Vol.1: Breakfast Recipes

Clean Eating Cookbook Vol.2: Lunch Recipes

Clean Eating Cookbook Vol.3: Dinner Recipes

Clean Eating Smoothies: Healthy Recipes Supporting A Whole Foods Lifestyle

This book is assuming you have the knowledge you need about following a clean eating diet, but if you are a complete beginner let's go over the basics of the diet.

Clean eating is not a new fad diet that is designed to lose weight, but is a lifestyle that promotes eating whole foods with a focus on overall health. Processed foods are eliminated or heavily moderated to ensure you are eating food in its most natural state. Depending on how long you have been including boxes of processed food in your daily diet it might take a bit of time to get used to switching over to a more natural diet.

The great thing about clean eating is the fact it is not complicated. There are isn't a need to count calories or wonder how much protein you are getting being you are just focused on eating the right foods.

How you set up your diet is really up to you but here are some guidelines:

● Eat 3-5 times a day with the three main meals consisting of complex carbohydrates (sweet potatoes, rice, oatmeal, etc.), a lean protein source, plenty of vegetables and fruit. Snacks if included can be raw veggies, fruit, nuts, etc.

• Drink plenty of fresh water and enjoy a variety of teas. If you hate the "flavor" of plain water try fruit infused water instead. Here is one book I recommend:

Fruit Infused Water: 70 Vitamin Water Recipes To Finally Cure Tasteless H2O by Darrin Wiggins

• Reduce the amount of processed goods made with wheat flour, trans fats and excessive sugar. Also, refined vegetable oils should be avoided.

• Enjoy plenty of healthy fats like nuts, avocados, olive oil, etc.

• Dairy always seems to be that controversial subject. I found conflicting advice when it came to dairy so I would suggest you eat it if you want and choose as natural of varieties as possible or choose not to eat it at all.

The goal, remember, is to always eat food that has been tampered with the least. I would say block cheese would be fine at my house, but cheese that sprays out of a can would be off the list.

As you can see it really just comes down to not eating the things we probably already know we shouldn't be eating and choosing healthier foods. It can be difficult to do, but the easiest way to transition is to have some delicious recipes available so you never feel deprived. I hope that is what you discover inside today.

Now let's get to eating!

Charity

Clean Eating Cookbook

Vol.1

Breakfast Recipes

Carrot Cake Flavored Oatmeal

Sweet vanilla and freshly shredded carrots are mixed with wholesome oats for this breakfast dish.

Servings: 4

Ingredients:

½ c. carrots (shredded)

1 tsp. cinnamon (ground)

½ tsp. nutmeg

2/3 c. almond milk

1 tsp. vanilla extract

2/3 c. oats (dry)

Coconut flakes (toasted, as needed)

Raisins (as needed)

Walnuts (chopped, as needed)

Directions:

1. Add the carrots, cinnamon, nutmeg, milk, and vanilla extract to a medium-sized pan.

2. Set it to medium-high heat and let it start to boil. Add in the oats and turn the heat off. Let this sit for a few minutes until oatmeal is cooked.

3. Sprinkle with coconut flakes, raisins, and walnuts.

Simple Refrigerated Oatmeal

This recipe uses classic oats, Greek yogurt, chia seeds, and honey in a mix that you can refrigerate easily.

Servings: 2

Ingredients:

1 ½ tsp. chia seeds

1/3 c. milk

1 tsp. honey

¼ c. oats (old fashioned)

¼ c. plain yogurt (Greek)

½ tsp. cinnamon

½ c. applesauce (unsweetened)

Directions:

1. Add the chia seeds, milk, honey, oats, and yogurt to 2 jars that are about half a pint.

2. Screw the lid on and shake the jars enough to blend all the ingredients.

3. Unscrew the lid and add in half of the cinnamon and applesauce to each jar. Stir and screw the lids back on.

4. Place in the refrigerator overnight and the oatmeal is ready to serve the next day.

Super Clean Waffles (Whole Wheat)

Honey, cinnamon, vanilla, and almond milk are a huge part of the sweet taste of these waffles.

Servings: 4

Ingredients:

2 Tbsp. honey

2 tsp. cinnamon

2 egg whites

1 ¾ c. flour (whole wheat)

1 tsp. baking powder

1 tsp. vanilla extract

2 c. almond milk

Directions:

1. Warm the waffle iron.

2. In a large-sized bowl, mix together the honey, cinnamon, egg whites, flour, baking powder, vanilla extract, and almond milk. Use a whisk to stir the ingredients thoroughly.

3. Coat the waffle iron with cooking spray and pour half of the batter in. Close the lid and let them cook for approximately 5 minutes. Do the same for the remaining batter.

4. Serve.

Pumpkin Pie Style Oatmeal

Smooth pumpkin puree, spice, maple syrup, and pecans make this a deliciously healthy breakfast.

Servings: 4

Ingredients:

1 c. oats (dry, cooked)

4 egg whites

1 tsp. pie spice (pumpkin, no added sugar)

½ c. pumpkin puree

Maple syrup (as needed)

¼ c. pecans

Directions:

1. Use the package instructions to cook the dry oats. Wait until 5 minutes before they are done to add in the egg whites. Stir continuously.

2. Add in the pumpkin pie spice and pumpkin puree.

3. Divide the oat mixture up into 4 bowls. Drizzle maple syrup over each and then sprinkle the pecans on top. Serve.

Lemon Flavored Muffins

A hint of lemon, honey, and almond milk blend together to make these soft and delicious treats.

Servings: 20

Ingredients:

2 tsp. baking soda

2 c. flour (whole wheat, pastry)

½ c. honey

1 egg

¼ c. olive oil

½ c. applesauce (unsweetened)

½ c. blueberries

4 Tbsp. lemon zest (fresh)

2 tsp. lemon extract

¾ c. almond milk

Directions:

1. Preheat the oven to 350 degrees.

2. Place baking cup liners in the muffin tins.

3. Mix the baking soda and flour in a medium-sized bowl. Mix the honey, egg, olive oil, applesauce, blueberries, lemon zest, lemon extract, and almond milk in another bowl.

4. Add the dry ingredients in with the wet. Whisk again and then pour the batter into the muffin tins. Be sure to only fill each cup to the halfway point.

5. Put them in the oven to cook for about 20 minutes. Take them out, let them cool, and serve.

Zucchini and Egg Muffins

Fresh zucchini, scallions, oregano, eggs, and basil make up this tasty breakfast.

Servings: 12

Ingredients:

4 scallions (chopped)

½ of a zucchini (shredded)

½ of a red pepper (minced)

2 carrots (shredded)

¼ tsp. oregano

Pepper (as desired)

Sea salt (as desired)

4 eggs (whole)

½ tsp. basil

14 egg whites

Directions:

1. Preheat the oven to 375 degrees. Spray a muffin tin with cooking spray.

2. In a large-sized bowl, mix together the scallions, zucchini, red pepper, and carrots. Pour this mixture into the muffin tin and fill each about 2/3 of the way full.

3. Whisk together the oregano, pepper, sea salt, whole eggs, basil, and egg whites in a large-sized bowl.

4. Pour 1/3 cup of the mixture into each muffin cup.

5. Place in the oven to bake for about 30 minutes. Serve immediately.

French Toast Cinnamon Sticks

Nutmeg, cinnamon, milk, and French bread are drizzled in delicious and sweet maple syrup.

Servings: 24 sticks

Ingredients:

¼ tsp. cinnamon

6 egg whites

¼ tsp. nutmeg (ground)

1 c. milk

1 Tbsp. olive oil

6 slices of bread (whole wheat, French, cut each slice into 4 strips)

3 Tbsp. maple syrup (pure)

Directions:

1. Mix together the cinnamon, egg whites, nutmeg, and milk in a bowl that is shallow.

2. Add the oil to a large-sized skillet and set the heat to medium.

3. Take each piece of bread and set it in the egg mixture and soak both sides. Take it out and place it in the skillet. Do this for a few more pieces and let them cook for about 5 minutes on both sides. Place the bread strips on a serving plate. Repeat this process for the remaining strips.

4. Drizzle maple syrup over the pieces or serve as a dip.

Berry Delicious Granola Bars

Sweet agave nectar, vanilla, fresh strawberries, raspberries and wholesome granola make up this tasty treat.

Servings: 8

Ingredients:

1 c. granola (whole grain)

1 tsp. vanilla extract (pure)

3 c. yogurt (Greek, low fat)

1/3 c. agave nectar

1 c. strawberries

1 c. raspberries

Directions:

1. Cover the inside of an 8 x 8 inch baking pan with foil.

2. Take the granola and add it to the bottom of the pan. Spread it out to make an even layer. Set this aside for now.

3. Mix together the vanilla, yogurt, agave nectar, strawberries and raspberries in a blender. Make sure that it has a smooth texture.

4. Pour the mixture into the pan and be sure it is spread out evenly over the granola. Cover the pan with foil and set it in the freezer for about 4 hours.

5. Cut into bars and serve.

Spanish Style Scrambled Eggs

Oregano, saffron, bell peppers, tomatoes, and eggs make up this breakfast scramble.

Servings: 2

Ingredients:

½ tsp. paprika

6 egg whites

½ tsp. oregano

Saffron (crushed, as desired)

1 egg yolk

Sunflower oil (as needed)

1 plum tomato (chopped)

1 zucchini (chopped)

1 bell pepper (red, minced)

2 slices of bread (whole grain, cut into cubes)

Directions:

1. Whisk together the paprika, egg whites, oregano, saffron, and yolk. Set this aside for now.

2. Add the oil to a large-sized pan. Warm it over high heat. Add in the tomato, zucchini, bell pepper, and bread. Let this cook for approximately 3 minutes.

3. Add the egg mixture on top and stir continuously for 3 minutes.

Banana and Peanut Butter Crepes

Savory peanut butter is mixed with cinnamon, almond milk, and creamy banana.

Servings: 2

Ingredients:

¾ of a banana (medium, mashed)

¼ tsp. baking powder

Cinnamon (as desired)

Almond milk (as needed)

¾ c. whey powder (peanut butter)

Salt (as desired)

1 egg white

Directions:

1. Mix the banana, baking powder, cinnamon, peanut butter whey, salt, and egg white in a large-sized bowl. Add a little milk and mix, the batter has to be thinner than pancake batter, add milk as needed to get the right texture.

2. Coat a large-sized skillet with cooking spray and put it on medium heat.

3. Pour half the mixture into the pan and cook for about 3 minutes on each side. Repeat with remaining batter.

4. Serve.

Coconut and Blueberry Smoothie

Fresh blueberries, almonds, coconut milk, and bananas are blended together for a great morning meal.

Servings: 2

Ingredients:

1 c. blueberries (frozen)

1 Tbsp. almonds

½ c. water

¼ c. coconut milk (canned)

1 banana (medium, sliced)

Directions:

1. Mix together the blueberries, almonds, water, milk, and banana using a blender.

2. Make sure it has been blended until it is completely smooth.

3. Serve.

Crispy Cherry Pancakes

Vanilla, cinnamon, almonds, and fresh cherries blend together for this breakfast dish.

Servings: 4

Ingredients:

1 ½ Tbsp. butter (unsalted, divided)

1 tsp. vanilla extract

3 eggs (large)

½ c. milk (low fat)

1 Tbsp. sugar (granulated)

Cinnamon (ground, as desired)

½ c. flour (whole wheat, pastry)

2 c. sweet cherries (fresh, pits removed, cut in half)

¼ c. almonds (sliced)

Powdered sugar (as needed)

Directions:

1. Preheat the oven to 450 degrees. Add the butter (1 teaspoon) to an oven-safe pan. Set in the oven and let the butter melt.

2. In a small-sized pan, warm the remaining butter over medium heat. Pour this in a medium-sized bowl and add in the vanilla, eggs, and milk. Stir, then add the granulated sugar, cinnamon, and flour. Use a whisk to mix everything together.

3. Take the pan out of the oven and move it around to let the butter coat evenly. Pour the cherries into make one even layer. Add the batter next and then sprinkle the almonds on top.

4. Put the pan back in the oven and let it cook for about 20 minutes.

5. Take out of the oven. Let it cool and then cut it into 4 equal wedges. Sprinkle on a small amount of powdered sugar.

Potato and Kale Stir Fry

Juicy kale and savory potatoes are blended with shallots, horseradish, and fresh pepper.

Servings: 4

Ingredients:

8 c. kale leaves (torn)

½ tsp. pepper (ground)

1 shallot (medium, minced)

¼ tsp. salt

2 Tbsp. horseradish

2 c. potatoes (cooked, shredded)

3 Tbsp. olive oil (extra virgin)

Directions:

1. Place the kale in a large-sized bowl that is safe to use in the microwave. Cook for about 3 minutes at full power. Take it out, drain it, and then chop it once it has cooled.

2. In a large-sized bowl, mix together the pepper, shallot, salt, and horseradish. Add in the potatoes and the kale. Stir.

3. In large-sized pan, on medium heat, warm the oil. Add in the mixture of kale and potatoes to the pan. Use a spatula to spread it out evenly. Stir a few times while cooking the mixture for about 4 minutes.

4. Flatten the mixture back out and let it continue cooking for about 15 minutes.

5. Serve.

Greek Style Breakfast Omelet

Feta cheese is mixed with pepper, shallots, spinach, and eggs.

Servings: 2

Ingredients:

¼ c. spinach (cooked)

4 large eggs

2 scallions (sliced thin)

Pepper (fresh, ground, as desired)

½ c. feta cheese (crumbled)

2 Tbsp. dill (fresh, chopped)

2 tsp. olive oil (extra virgin)

Directions:

1. Take the spinach and squeeze it gently. This will help remove any extra water.

2. Use a fork to beat the eggs in a medium-sized bowl. Add in the scallions, pepper, feta, spinach, and dill. Mix using a spatula that is rubber.

3. Place a rack approximately 4 inches away from the element and turn the broiler on.

4. Use a large-sized, oven safe pan and warm the oil on medium heat. Add the mixture of eggs in and make sure it is an even layer. Set the heat to medium-low and let this cook for about 4 minutes.

5. Put the pan in the oven to broil for about two and half minutes. Take the omelet out and let it cool for a few minutes. Slice into wedges and serve.

Mushroom Onion Egg Scramble

This recipe has a mix of onions, garlic, mushrooms, basil, tomatoes, eggs, and spinach.

Servings: 6

Ingredients:

1 ½ c. asparagus (fresh)

2 tsp. olive oil

1 c. mushrooms (fresh, chopped)

2 garlic cloves (minced)

¼ c. onions (chopped)

3 c. spinach (fresh, chopped)

¼ c. tomatoes (sun-dried, chopped)

½ c. fresh basil (chopped)

6 egg whites

Directions:

1. Add the asparagus to a medium-sized pan. Pour in enough water to cover and let it boil. Once the asparagus is a brighter color, take it out. Add ice and water to a bowl and place the asparagus in it to cool. Drain and chop into pieces.

2. In a large-sized skillet, on medium heat, warm the oil. Toss in the mushrooms, garlic, and onions. Let them cook for approximately 5 minutes. Add the asparagus and spinach and cook for about 5 minutes.

3. Add the tomatoes, basil, and egg whites. Stir continuously for about 5 minutes.

Easy and Clean Breakfast Bars

Figs, raisins, oats, vanilla, honey, almonds, apricots, and pecans make up this great breakfast boost.

Servings: 24

Ingredients:

Cooking spray (olive oil)

1 c. figs (dried)

1 c. almonds (sliced)

1 c. pecans (chopped)

½ c. apricots (dried, sliced in half)

1 ½ c. rice cereal (brown)

1 ½ c. oats

½ c. raisins (packed)

1 tsp. vanilla extract

¼ c. honey

3 egg whites

½ tsp. cinnamon

¼ tsp. sea salt

Directions:

1. Preheat the oven to 350 degrees. Coat a 9 x 13 pan using cooking spray.

2. Place the figs, almonds, pecans, and apricots in a food processor and process until everything is chopped evenly. Put this mixture in a large-sized bowl.

3. Add the cereal, oats and raisins in and stir.

4. Mix the vanilla, honey, egg whites, cinnamon and salt in a different bowl. Stir then pour into the bowl with the figs mixture. Stir.

5. Pour this mix in the pan and press on it softly. Put it in the oven and let it bake for about 25 minutes.

6. Take out of the oven and let it cool for about 30 minutes before cutting the mixture into 24 bars.

Cinnamon French Toast

Whole wheat bread, cinnamon, milk, and nutmeg make up this easy breakfast meal.

Servings: 20

Ingredients:

¼ tsp. cinnamon (ground)

¼ tsp. nutmeg (ground)

6 egg whites

1 c. milk (organic, fat-free)

20 slices of bread (whole wheat, French)

2 Tbsp. olive oil

Directions:

1. In a medium-sized bowl, mix together the cinnamon, nutmeg, eggs, and milk. Dip the bread into the mixture and let it soak into each side.

2. Add the oil to a medium-sized pan and warm it on medium-heat. Brown each side of the bread slices, then place them on a serving tray. Sprinkle with sugar and drizzle on the honey.

Protein Packed Peanut Butter Bars

Oats, protein powder, peanut butter and almond milk make up this super easy breakfast bars.

Servings: 6

Ingredients:

½ c. peanut butter

½ c. almond milk (unsweetened)

2 c. oats

4 scoops of protein powder (vanilla)

Directions:

1. Place wax paper inside a glass baking pan that is 8 x 8 inches.

2. In a medium-sized bowl, mix together the peanut butter, almond milk, oats, and protein powder using your hands.

3. Add the mixture to the baking pan. Take a spatula and press the mixture flat. Put this in the freezer for about 30 minutes.

4. Take the pan out of the freezer and slice mixture into 6 bars. Set in the refrigerator until ready to serve.

Strawberry Vanilla Pancakes

This pancake recipe blends together strawberries, vanilla, coconut milk, and applesauce.

Servings: 5

Ingredients:

2 Tbsp. water

7 strawberries (medium, remove the stems, cut into quarters)

2/3 c. applesauce (unsweetened)

1 tsp. vanilla extract

½ c. yogurt (plain, Greek, unsweetened)

2 egg whites

2/3 c. coconut milk

1 ¼ c. oat flour (gluten free)

¼ tsp. baking powder

Directions:

1. Mix together the water and strawberries in a medium-sized pan and put the pan over medium heat. Let it boil then stir the strawberries often. Let them cook for about 5 minutes.

2. In a large-sized bowl, add in the applesauce, vanilla extract, yogurt, egg whites, and coconut milk. Whisk to combine. Add the flour and baking powder and stir again.

3. Take the pan away from the heat and mash the strawberries. Add them to the applesauce mixture and stir to combine.

4. Warm oil in a medium-sized saucepan on medium heat. Pour part of the mixture in and let it cook for about 3 minutes on each side. Place on a serving plate. Do this for the remainder of the batter.

5. Serve.

Sweet Banana Bread

Bananas are mixed with cinnamon, sugar, fresh egg whites, and a little bit of sea salt.

Servings: 8

Ingredients:

Olive oil (as needed)

1 c. bananas (ripe, peeled, mashed)

½ tsp. cinnamon (ground)

Sea salt (as desired)

1 ½ c. pastry flour (whole wheat)

½ tsp. baking soda

1 ¼ tsp. baking powder

¼ c. coconut oil

½ c. sugar (sucanat)

2 egg whites (beaten)

Directions:

1. Preheat the oven to 350 degrees.

2. Use olive oil to coat a loaf pan that is 8x4x2 inch.

3. Place the bananas in a bowl and set them aside.

4. Mix the cinnamon, salt, flour, baking soda, and baking powder in a separate bowl.

5. Add the coconut oil, sugar, and egg whites to the bowl with the bananas. Stir to mix well. Add the cinnamon mixture in and stir gently.

6. Add the mixture to the loaf pan and put it in the oven. Let it bake for about 50 minutes.

7. Take the bread out and let it cool for about 15 minutes. Slice and serve.

Protein Boosted Blueberry Muffins

Bananas, vanilla, cinnamon, and protein powder are blended with fresh blueberries.

Servings: 12

Ingredients:

3 Tbsp. almond milk (unsweetened)

2 ½ c. protein powder

1 banana (mashed)

1 ½ c. egg whites

2 Tbsp. flaxseed (ground)

2 Tbsp. water

¼ c. apple sauce (no added sugar, organic)

1 tsp. vanilla extract

3 tsp. baking powder

3 tbsp. flour (almond)

2 Tbsp. coconut oil (warmed)

1 ½ Tbsp. cinnamon

Sea salt (as desired)

½ c. blueberries

Directions:

1. Preheat the oven to 350 degrees.

2. Add the milk and banana to a large bowl. Whisk together and add in the egg whites, flaxseed, water, applesauce, vanilla extract, baking powder, flour, oil, cinnamon, and sea salt. Stir gently to mix. Softly stir in the blueberries.

3. Add baking cups to the muffin tin and pour the mixture in. Place in the oven to bake for about 20 minutes.

4. Take the muffins out and let them cool. Serve.

Cinnamon Sprinkled Grapefruit

Cinnamon, honey, and nutmeg and mixed with deliciously fresh grapefruit.

Servings: 1

Ingredients:

1 grapefruit

½ tsp. of vanilla (extract)

1 Tbsp. pure honey

Nutmeg (as desired)

Cardamom (as desired)

Cinnamon (as desired)

Directions:

1. Place an oven rack about 4 inches from the broiler and set the oven to broil.

2. Slice the grapefruit. Use two small-sized baking pans to place the grapefruit in. Pour some vanilla and honey on top of each half. Sprinkle some nutmeg, cardamom, and cinnamon on each half.

3. Place the grapefruit in the oven to bake for about 5 minutes.

4. Take them out and let them cool for just a few minutes before serving.

Banana and Strawberry Breakfast Bars

This granola bar recipe uses honey, milk, bananas, and fresh strawberries.

Servings: 10

Ingredients:

½ banana (large, mashed)

½ c. milk (skim)

1 tsp. oil (coconut, melted)

1 Tbsp. pure honey

2 ½ c. oats (old fashioned)

1 c. strawberries (frozen, unsweetened, diced)

Directions:

1. Preheat the oven to 300 degrees. Spray an 8 x 8 baking dish using cooking spray.

2. Mix the banana, milk, coconut oil, and honey in a large-sized bowl. Add in the oats and stir. Add the strawberries and softly stir them into the mix.

3. Pour the mixture into the pan and press it down gently. Put the dish into the oven and let it bake for about 19 minutes.

4. Take the dish out and let it cool before cutting the mixture into 10 bars.

5. Place plastic wrap over the dish and let it refrigerate until just before serving.

Banana Bread Flavored Granola

Cinnamon, bananas, oats, pecans, and walnuts, make this a great dish for breakfast.

Servings: 12

Ingredients:

½ c. pecans

¾ c. walnuts

½ tsp. sea salt

½ Tbsp. cinnamon

1 Tbsp. flaxseed

3 Tbsp. sugar (raw)

3 c. oats (rolled)

¼ c. coconut oil

1 tsp. vanilla extract

1/3 c. maple syrup

1 banana (medium, ripe, peeled, mashed)

Directions:

1. Preheat the oven to 350 degrees.

2. In a large-sized bowl, mix together the pecans, walnuts, salt, cinnamon, flaxseed, sugar, and oats.

3. Add the coconut oil to a small-sized pan and warm it on medium-low. Add in the vanilla extract and maple syrup. Stir. After everything has melted completely, take it away from the heat.

4. Add the mashed bananas in and stir. Pour this mixture in with the nut mixture. Stir to combine everything thoroughly.

5. Divide the mixture up between two baking sheets and spread it into a thin layer on each. Set it in the oven and let it bake for about 28 minutes, stirring occasionally to break up some of the clumps. It should be a golden color when it is ready.

6. Take the pans out of the oven and shake them around a little to loosen it up a bit. Let it cool entirely before placing it in a container to store.

Sunflower and Honey Granola

Delicious sunflower seeds are mixed with almonds, cranberries, vanilla, and honey in this granola dish.

Servings: 8

Ingredients:

1 ½ c. oatmeal

½ c. cranberries (dried)

½ c. coconut (shredded, unsweetened)

½ tsp. sea salt

½ tsp. vanilla extract (pure)

¾ c. sunflower seeds

½ c. slivered almonds

¼ c. flaxseed (ground)

3 Tbsp. peanut butter (natural)

1/3 c. honey (raw)

Directions:

1. Preheat the oven to 300 degrees.

2. Mix together the oatmeal, cranberries, coconut, sea salt, vanilla extract, sunflower seeds, flaxseeds, almonds, peanut butter, and honey in a large-sized bowl.

3. Add the mixture to a large enough baking dish and press it in tightly. Bake for about 40 minutes.

4. Take the dish out and let the granola cool. Serve.

Onion Black Bean Burrito

This breakfast burrito recipe has an array of flavors from onions, black beans, green peppers, eggs, tomatoes, and cottage cheese.

Servings: 4

Ingredients:

4 tortillas (small, whole wheat)

Black pepper (fresh, as desired)

½ c. cottage cheese (nonfat)

Sea salt (as desired)

2 c. egg whites

½ c. onions (sweet, chopped)

½ c. green peppers (sweet, chopped)

½ c. tomatoes (chopped)

½ c. black beans (rinsed, drained)

Directions:

1. Preheat the oven to 170 degrees. Set the tortillas on a baking pan and let them warm in the oven.

2. Whisk together the pepper, cottage cheese, salt, and egg whites in a small-sized bowl.

3. Spray cooking spray in a medium-sized pan and let it warm over medium heat. Add in the onions, green peppers, tomatoes, and black beans.

4. Add the cottage cheese mixture in and let it cook. Once it is has set, take the tortillas out of the oven and place some of the mixture into each.

5. Roll them up and serve.

Cranberry Blueberry Muffins

Blueberries are mixed with cranberry, sugar, vanilla, and cinnamon.

Servings: 12

Ingredients:

1 tsp. baking soda

2 c. flour (whole wheat)

2 tsp. baking powder

1 tsp. cinnamon

½ c. cranberries

1 c. blueberries (frozen)

4 egg whites

3 bananas (mashed)

½ c. applesauce (unsweetened)

1 tsp. vanilla extract

1/3 c. sugar (raw)

Directions:

1. Preheat the oven to 350 degrees. Place baking cups inside a muffin tin.

2. Mix together the baking soda, flour, baking powder, and cinnamon in a large-sized bowl. Add in the cranberries and blueberries and softly stir them to coat.

3. Mix together the egg whites, bananas, applesauce, vanilla, and sugar in a medium-sized bowl. Add this mixture into the flour mixture. Stir.

4. Pour the batter into the individual cups of the muffin tin. Place them in the oven to bake for about 22 minutes.

Fruit Mix French Toast

Blueberries are mixed with strawberries, chia seeds, vanilla, and cinnamon.

Servings: 2

Ingredients:

1 tsp. vanilla extract (pure)

1 tsp. cinnamon

3 egg whites

1 tsp. nutmeg

¼ c. milk (skim)

2 slices of bread (whole grain)

1 Tbsp. powdered sugar (organic)

2 Tbsp. chia seeds

1 Tbsp. honey (raw)

½ c. strawberries

½ c. blueberries

Directions:

1. Mix together the vanilla, cinnamon, egg whites, nutmeg, and milk in a medium-sized bowl. Set the bread in the mixture and let it soak for about 1 minute on each side.

2. Coat a nonstick pan with cooking spray. Place it on medium heat and add the bread in. Cook for approximately 3 minutes per side. It should be golden in color.

3. Place each piece on a plate and sprinkle some sugar and chia seeds on top. Drizzle some honey on and add some strawberries and blueberries.

Smooth Strawberry Breakfast Shake

Fresh strawberries are mixed with deliciously sweet vanilla almond milk for a quick and tasty breakfast.

Servings: 1

Ingredients:

4 strawberries (fresh, large, sliced in half)

¼ c. coconut milk (unsweetened)

½ c. strawberries (frozen, unsweetened)

¾ c. almond milk (vanilla flavored)

Directions:

1. Place the fresh strawberries in a small-sized bowl. Use a fork to mash them as much as possible. Add this into a large cup.

2. Add in the coconut milk, frozen strawberries and almond milk.

3. Blend the ingredients together using a hand blender.

Banana and Applesauce Waffles

Fresh bananas and applesauce are blended with cinnamon, vanilla, and the sweet taste of almond milk.

Servings: 6

Ingredients:

2 bananas (ripe)

2 eggs

½ c. applesauce (unsweetened)

1 ½ c. almond milk

½ tsp. cinnamon

1 Tbsp. baking powder

1 c. oats

1 tsp. vanilla

½ tsp. salt

1 c. flour (whole wheat)

Honey (raw)

Directions:

1. Warm the waffle iron.

2. Add the bananas to a medium-sized bowl and use a fork to mash them. They should be a very smooth texture. Add in the eggs and applesauce. Use a whisk to stir.

3. Pour the milk in and stir again.

4. Add the cinnamon, baking powder, oats, vanilla, salt, and wheat flour. Stir and make sure everything is blended thoroughly.

5. Pour some batter into the waffle iron and close the lid. Let them cook long enough to be a golden brown color. Repeat with remaining batter.

6. Serve drizzled with raw honey.

Quinoa Berry Mix

Quinoa is blended with honey, vanilla, berries, and cinnamon.

Servings: 4

Ingredients:

1 c. quinoa (organic, rinsed)

1 c. water

1 c. almond milk

1 tsp. cinnamon

2 c. mixed berries (fresh blueberries, strawberries, and raspberries)

1 tsp. vanilla

¼ c. almonds (chopped)

4 tsp. honey

Directions:

1. In a medium-sized pan, add the quinoa, water, and milk. Set it on high heat and let it start to boil.

2. Set the heat on medium-low and let it simmer for about 15 minutes. Take it away from the heat and cover. Let this sit for about 5 minutes.

3. Uncover and stir in the cinnamon, berries, and vanilla. Divide the mixture up into 4 separate serving bowls and then sprinkle some almonds on top. Drizzle some honey over each bowl and serve.

Pumpkin Oat Pancakes

Smooth pumpkin is mixed with vanilla, oats, and spice and topped with sweet maple syrup.

Servings: 4

Ingredients:

1 c. oats (rolled, whole)

½ c. cottage cheese

6 egg whites

1 tsp. pumpkin pie spice

1 tsp. vanilla

¼ c. pumpkin (canned)

Maple syrup (pure, as needed)

Directions:

1. In a large-sized bowl, mix together the pumpkin spice, oats, cottage cheese, egg whites, vanilla, and pumpkin.

2. Coat a medium-sized pan with cooking spray and pour ¼ of the batter into the pan. Cook for about 3 minutes on each side and place on a serving plate. Repeat this process for the remaining batter.

3. Drizzle maple syrup on top and serve.

Egg White Spinach Muffins

Egg whites, spinach, peppers, and mushrooms are mixed together for this muffin recipe.

Servings: 6 large muffins

Ingredients:

1 egg (whole)

¼ c. green and red pepper (chopped)

½ c. mushrooms (chopped)

Mrs. Dash (Salt Free, as desired)

8 egg whites

½ c. spinach (chopped)

¼ c. onion

Directions:

1. Preheat the oven to 350 degrees.

2. Place the egg, peppers, mushrooms, seasoning, egg whites, spinach, and onions in a blender. Blend enough to mix everything thoroughly.

3. Place baking cups in the muffin tin and pour mixture into each cup until full. Place in the oven to bake for about 15 minutes.

4. Take them out and let them cool for approximately 10 minutes. Serve.

Raisin Maple Oatmeal

Oats are blended together with milk, cinnamon, ginger, and tasty raisins.

Servings: 4

Ingredients:

1 tsp. ginger (ground)

¼ c. maple syrup

½ c. raisins

1 tsp. cinnamon (ground)

¼ c. milk

1 c. oats (old fashioned, rolled)

Directions:

1. In a large-sized pan, mix together the ginger, maple syrup, raisins, cinnamon, milk, and oats. Set it over medium-high heat and let it start to boil.

2. Lower the heat down to low. Simmer for about 5 minutes. Serve.

Broccoli Egg Scramble

Broccoli is cooked with eggs, brown rice, and a pinch of soy sauce.

Servings: 1

Ingredients:

2 c. broccoli (chopped, steamed)

1 c. cooked brown rice

½ tsp. soy sauce

2 egg whites

1 egg

Directions:

1. After steaming the broccoli, drain it and return into the pan.

2. Add in the rice, soy sauce, egg whites, and egg. Place pan on medium heat, stirring continuously until the eggs are scrambled completely.

3. Serve immediately.

Blueberry Breakfast Spinach Smoothie

Fresh blueberries are blended together with cinnamon and spinach.

Servings: 1

Ingredients:

¼ tsp. cinnamon

1 c. water

1 c. spinach

1 Tbsp. flaxseed

1 c. blueberries

Directions:

1. Add the cinnamon, water, spinach, flaxseed, and blueberries to a blender. Blend until completely smooth.

2. Serve at room temperature or chilled.

Tomato Egg Breakfast Bakes

Tomatoes are stuffed with fresh basil, eggs, and sprinkled with a little bit of salt and pepper.

Servings: 6

Ingredients:

6 tomatoes (medium)

3 eggs (organic, free ranged)

4 leaves of basil (chopped)

Black pepper (as desired)

Sea salt (as desired)

Directions:

1. Preheat the oven to 350 degrees.

2. Slice off the top of the tomatoes. Remove the insides. Set each tomato inside the cups in a muffin pan.

3. Add the eggs to a medium-sized bowl and whisk to blend them thoroughly.

4. Divide the basil up and place in each tomato cup. Divide the egg mixture up and pour into each tomato cup.

5. Place the muffin pan in the oven to cook for approximately 30 minutes. Take them out and sprinkle pepper and salt over them.

6. Serve.

Clean Eating Cookbook

Vol.2

Lunch Recipes

Classic Chicken Salad with A Twist

This is a blend of celery, grapes, yogurt, fresh chicken breasts, garlic, and romaine lettuce.

Servings: 4

Ingredients:

1 tsp. black pepper (fresh, ground)

½ c. yogurt (Greek, nonfat)

¼ onion (red, chopped)

2 chicken breasts (organic, cooked and sliced into cubes)

Sea salt (as desired)

1 tsp. garlic powder

½ c. red grapes (seedless, cut into quarters)

4 lettuce leaves (romaine, chopped)

2 stalks of celery (chopped)

Directions:

1. Mix together the pepper, yogurt, onions, chicken, salt, garlic powder, grapes, lettuce, and celery using a large-sized bowl.

2. Serve immediately or chill for a few hours.

Spicy Tuna Salad

The classic taste of tuna, celery, onions, and fresh mayonnaise with a bit of kick.

Servings: 4

Ingredients:

¼ c. onions (red, diced thin)

Sea salt (as desired)

1 stalk of celery (large, sliced thin)

1/3 c. mayonnaise (organic)

Dried chili flakes to taste (crushed)

2 cans of tuna (packed in water, drained)

Directions:

1. Mix together the onions, sea salt, celery, mayonnaise, chili flakes and tuna in a medium-sized bowl.

2. Serve as is or chilled.

Garlic Chickpeas with Parmesan

Chickpeas are baked with the goodness of garlic, sea salt, and savory parmesan cheese.

Servings: 2

Ingredients:

2 15oz. cans of chickpeas (drained, rinsed)

Black pepper (fresh, ground, as desired)

½ tsp. sea salt

1 Tbsp. olive oil

1 tsp. garlic (minced)

½ c. parmesan cheese (grated)

Directions:

1. Lay paper towels out on a clean surface and place the chickpeas on top. Let them sit for about 30 minutes to dry.

2. Preheat the oven to 400 degrees.

3. Mix together the pepper, salt, oil, and garlic in a medium-sized bowl. Add in the cheese and stir. Crumbles should start to form.

4. Add the chickpeas in and stir to make sure they are evenly coated.

5. Place the chickpeas on a baking pan, in an even layer. Set them in the oven and let them bake for about 50 minutes.

6. Serve.

Garlic and Onion Stuffed Zucchini

Zucchini stuffed with onions, garlic, bread crumbs, and drizzled with delicious balsamic vinegar.

Servings: 4

Ingredients:

3 tsp. olive oil (divided)

8 oz. of mushrooms (diced)

1 onion (small, yellow, diced)

1 garlic clove (diced)

2 Tbsp. parmesan cheese

1 Tbsp. vinegar (balsamic)

3 Tbsp. bread crumbs (whole wheat)

2 zucchini (cut in half, seeds removed, pulp removed)

Directions:

1. Preheat the oven to 350 degrees.

2. Add the oil (1 teaspoon) to a large-sized skillet. Set the heat to medium-high. Toss in the mushrooms, onions, and garlic. Stir and let them sauté for approximately 10 minutes.

3. Take the skillet off the heat and add in the remainder of the oil. Place the parmesan, vinegar, and bread crumbs in next. Stir to make sure everything is blended well.

4. Divide the mixture up and place it within each zucchini. Place foil on a baking pan and set the zucchinis on it.

5. Place them in the oven to bake for about 10 minutes.

Chickpea Moroccan Style Salad

Cumin, sea salt, chickpeas, onions, feta cheese, and carrots make up this tasty salad dish.

Servings: 6

Ingredients:

2 tsp. cumin

¼ tsp. black pepper (ground)

3 Tbsp. lemon juice (fresh)

3 Tbsp. olive oil

Cayenne pepper (as desired)

¼ tsp. sea salt

1 carrot (large, peeled, sliced)

2 tomatoes (plum, diced)

1 bell pepper (red, diced)

¼ c. mint (fresh, chopped)

3 c. chickpeas (drained, rinsed)

1/3 c. feta cheese (low fat, crumbled)

3 onions (green, sliced thin)

¼ c. cilantro (fresh, chopped)

Directions:

1. Add the cumin, black pepper, lemon juice, oil, cayenne, and salt to a small-sized bowl. Whisk everything together to make the dressing.

2. Add the carrots, tomatoes, bell pepper, mint, chickpeas, feta, onions and cilantro to a large-sized bowl.

3. Drizzle the lemon dressing on top of the chickpea mix and stir gently to coat everything.

4. Serve at room temperature or chill for a few hours in the refrigerator.

Cucumber Crab Quinoa Salad

Crab is blended together with delicious wine vinegar, cilantro, soy sauce, and cucumbers.

Servings: 4

Ingredients:

1 c. quinoa

2 cucumbers (English, seedless, sliced)

1 tsp. sesame oil

2 Tbsp. soy sauce (low sodium, organic)

2 Tbsp. vinegar (rice wine)

1 tsp. lemon juice

8 oz. of crabmeat (fresh)

1 Tbsp. cilantro (fresh, chopped)

Directions:

1. Use the package instructions to cook the quinoa. Let it cool.

2. Put the cucumbers in a medium-sized bowl.

3. Mix together the oil, soy sauce, and vinegar using a small-sized bowl. Drizzle the mixture over the cucumbers. Stir gently to coat.

4. Separate the quinoa onto 4 serving plates. Divide the cucumbers up and place them on top of the quinoa.

5. Mix the lemon juice and crab meat together in a small-sized bowl. Divide this up and put it on top of the cucumbers.

6. Set the plates in the refrigerator to chill for about 3 hours. Sprinkle cilantro on top and serve.

Wakame and Shrimp Salad

Wakame seaweed is served alongside juicy shrimp, celery, green onions, and soy sauce.

Servings: 4

Ingredients:

4 quarts of water

16 oz. of shrimp (shells removed, veins removed)

2 Tbsp. wakame seaweed (soak in cold water for 5 minutes, chopped)

2 onions (green, sliced)

2 ribs of celery (sliced)

1 tsp. sesame oil

2 Tbsp. soy sauce (reduced sodium, organic)

¼ c. vinegar (rice wine)

Directions:

1. Add the water to a large enough pan and set the heat to medium-high. Bring water to a boil. Toss the shrimp in and let them cook for approximately 1 minute or until cooked. Take the shrimp out and run cold water over them to rinse. Drain and place in a large-sized bowl.

2. Add in the wakame, onions, and celery. Stir gently to combine.

3. Using a whisk, mix together the oil, soy sauce, and vinegar in a small-sized bowl. Drizzle this on top of the shrimp salad and stir gently.

4. Set in the refrigerator for about 3 hours. Serve.

Tuna and Cabbage Salad

Tuna, cabbage, onions, almonds, and sesame seeds blend together with a wine vinegar dressing.

Servings: 4

Ingredients:

2 c. red cabbage (shredded)

2 Tbsp. almonds (sliced)

2 tsp. sesame seeds

3 c. Napa cabbage (shredded)

2 onions (green, sliced)

12 oz. of tuna (packed in water and drained)

1 Tbsp. olive oil

1 Tbsp. sucanat

3 Tbsp. vinegar (rice wine)

Sea salt (as desired)

1 tsp. sesame oil

Directions:

1. Using a large-sized bowl, mix together the red cabbage, almonds, sesame seeds, Napa cabbage, and onions. Gently stir in the tuna.

2. Use a whisk, and a small-sized bowl, to blend the olive oil, sucanat, vinegar, sea salt, and sesame oil. Drizzle the mixture in with the tuna mix. Gently stir again.

3. Chill for 3 hours before serving.

Mushroom and Pearl Barley Risotto

This risotto recipe mixes garlic, barley, parsley, onions, and thyme.

Servings: 6

Ingredients:

5 c. chicken broth

1 Tbsp. butter

1 onion (chopped)

1 bay leaf

¾ tsp. thyme (dried)

1 c. barley (pearl)

1 Tbsp. olive oil

1 lb. mushrooms (sliced)

2 cloves of garlic (chopped)

2 Tbsp. parsley (fresh, chopped)

Directions:

1. Add the chicken broth to a pot and let it boil over medium-high heat.

2. Warm the butter to a large-sized pan and set the heat to medium. Toss in the onions and let them simmer for about 5 minutes. Add in the bay leaf, thyme, barley and 2 cups chicken broth. Lower the heat to low and let it continue to cook for about 10 minutes.

3. Add the remainder of the broth. Cook on low stirring occasionally until the broth is absorbed. It takes approximately 50 minutes.

4. Add the olive oil to a large-sized skillet. Toss in the mushrooms and cook for a couple of minutes. Add the garlic and continue cooking for approximately 3 minutes. Add the barley and parsley.

5. Take the bay leaf out and it's ready to serve.

Crispy Chicken Nuggets

Fresh chicken breasts are coated in delicious flavors of basil, thyme, parsley, black pepper, and red pepper.

Servings: 4

Ingredients:

1 Tbsp. water

2 eggs (beaten)

4 chicken breasts (organic, skinless, boneless, fat trimmed, cut into cubes)

1 tsp. black pepper (ground)

½ c. wheat germ

Red pepper flakes (crushed, as desired)

1 tsp. parsley (fresh, chopped)

1 tsp. basil (dried)

½ c. bread crumbs (whole wheat, seasoned)

½ tsp. thyme (dried)

1 Tbsp. vegetable oil

Directions:

1. Preheat the oven to 425 degrees. Coat a baking pan with cooking spray.

2. Add the water and eggs to a large-sized bowl. Beat the eggs into the water then add in the chicken.

3. In a separate large-sized bowl, mix together the pepper, wheat germ, red pepper, parsley, basil, bread crumbs, and thyme. Add the oil and stir it in using a fork. Add this mixture to a large bag that you can securely seal.

4. Place the chicken in the bag and toss to coat the chicken. Set the chicken on the baking pan and put it in the oven. Let it bake for about 10 minutes. Flip the pieces over and continue baking for 5 minutes or until done.

Spinach Salad with Strawberries

This salad is a blend of onions, strawberries, paprika, vinegar, spinach, and almonds.

Servings: 4

Ingredients:

¼ tsp. paprika

½ c. olive oil

1 Tbsp. poppy seeds

¼ c. white vinegar (distilled)

½ c. sugar (raw, organic)

¼ tsp. Worcestershire sauce

2 Tbsp. sesame seeds

¼ c. almonds (blanched, slivered)

10 oz. of spinach (fresh, rinsed, dried, chopped)

1 Tbsp. onion (minced)

1 qt. strawberries (fresh, stems removed, sliced)

Directions:

1. Use a whisk to mix together the paprika, olive oil, poppy seeds, vinegar, sugar, Worcestershire sauce, and sesame seeds in a medium-sized bowl. Cover the bowl and let it sit in the refrigerator for about 1 hour.

2. Mix together the almonds, spinach, onions, and strawberries in a large-sized bowl. Pour the dressing mixture on top of the salad. Gently stir to coat everything. Put the salad in the refrigerator to chill for about 15 minutes.

Carrots Served with Mango Chutney Glaze

Baby carrots are cooked with delicious Dijon mustard, mango Chutney, and sea salt.

Servings: 4

Ingredients:

1 lb. carrots (baby)

2 tsp. butter (organic, grass fed)

¼ tsp. sea salt

2 tsp. Dijon mustard (whole grain)

¼ c. mango chutney (organic)

Directions:

1. Put the carrots inside a large-sized pan and fill it with enough water to cover them completely. Set the heat to medium-high and let it start to boil.

2. Lower the heat and let the carrots simmer for about 10 minutes. Drain the carrots. Place them back in the pan and add in the butter, sea salt, mustard, and chutney.

3. Continue to sauté them for about 2 minutes. Serve.

Fennel and Watermelon Salad

Fresh watermelon is tossed with honey, black pepper, mint, fennel, and shallots.

Servings: 8

Ingredients:

¼ tsp. black pepper (fresh, ground)

1 Tbsp. honey (organic)

3 Tbsp. lime juice (fresh)

¼ tsp. salt (Kosher)

2 Tbsp. olive oil

1 Tbsp. shallots (minced)

3 c. watermelon (fresh, cubed)

3 ¼ c. fennel bulbs (sliced thin)

2 oz. feta cheese (crumbled)

¼ c. mint (fresh, chopped)

Directions:

1. Mix together the black pepper, honey, lime juice, salt, and olive oil, using a whisk. Add the shallots and stir again.

2. Using a large-sized bowl, mix together the watermelon and fennel. Pour the dressing on top and softly stir. Add the cheese and mint on top and serve.

Lemon Tofu Drizzled Cucumber Salad

Tomatoes, cucumbers, lettuce, onions, black olives, and feta cheese are blended with a lemon infused tofu dressing.

Servings: 6

Ingredients:

½ c. black olives (drained, sliced, pits removed)

1 c. red onion (sliced into thin rings)

2 c. tomatoes (seeds removed, chopped)

1 c. edamame (shells removed, cooked)

1 ½ c. romaine lettuce (torn)

3 c. cucumbers (peeled, chopped)

1 ½ c. iceberg lettuce (torn)

¼ tsp. salt

½ tsp. oregano leaves (dried)

1 Tbsp. lemon juice

12 oz. tofu (silken)

½ tsp. black pepper (fresh, ground)

1 tsp. garlic (minced)

2 Tbsp. olive oil (extra virgin)

Feta cheese (crumbled, as desired)

Directions:

1. Use a large sized bowl and mix together the olives, onions, tomatoes, edamame, romaine lettuce, cucumbers, and iceberg lettuce.

2. Add the salt, oregano, lemon juice, tofu, pepper, garlic, and oil into a food processor. Let it blend until it is completely smooth.

3. Drizzle the dressing on top of the salad and stir together gently. Add the feta cheese on top of and serve.

Cajun Style Mixed Bean Soup

A mix of beans, onions, peppers, celery, and garlic are served as a delicious and refreshing soup

Servings: 8

Ingredients:

12 c. water

20 oz. of mixed beans (rinsed, dried)

1 bell pepper (chopped)

1 celery rib (chopped)

1 garlic clove (minced)

1 onion (large, chopped)

1 lemon (for juice)

½ tsp. oregano

¼ tsp. cayenne pepper

2 tsp. paprika

1 tsp. thyme

1 tsp. chili powder

15 oz. can of tomatoes (stewed)

1 ½ tsp. sea salt

½ tsp. smoke flavoring (liquid)

Directions:

1. Add water (12 cups) to a large pot. Add the beans and then set it on medium high heat. Let it boil then reduce to medium heat. Let this cook for about 75 minutes. The beans should be soft but not mushy.

2. Add the bell pepper, celery, garlic, and onions to a large-sized skillet. Let them cook over medium-high heat, enough to brown. Add this mixture in with beans.

3. Add in the lemon juice, oregano, cayenne pepper, paprika, thyme, chili powder, and tomatoes. Continue cooking for about 45 minutes.

4. Add the salt and liquid smoke. Stir and serve.

Creamy Goat Cheese Pear Salad

Salad greens, balsamic vinegar, walnuts, and goat cheese are tossed together to make this tasty lunch salad.

Servings: 8

Ingredients:

¼ c. walnuts

4 c. salad greens (washed)

4 pears

2 oz. cheese (goat)

1 Tbsp. olive oil (extra virgin)

2 Tbsp. vinegar (balsamic)

Directions:

1. Add the walnuts to a small-sized skillet and roast them on medium heat for about 5 minutes. Take them out and chop them up.

2. Place the salad greens (about 1/2 cup) on each serving plate.

3. Cut each pear in half. Take each pear half and scoop out a ball shape in the center. Take the cheese and slice it. Round each slice into the shape of a ball. Place the cheese balls in the walnuts and roll them around to coat. Put the balls inside each hollowed out pear half. Set the pears on top of the lettuce.

4. In a small bowl, whisk together the oil and vinegar until it is a smooth texture. Sprinkle some of this mixture and some of the remaining walnuts on top of each pear half. Serve.

Garlic Turkey Meatballs

Juicy turkey is mixed with onions, parsley, basil, oregano, garlic, and a sprinkling of sea salt.

Servings: 20

Ingredients:

2 Tbsp. basil (chopped fine)

2 garlic cloves (pressed)

½ c. onion (finely chopped)

1 tsp. sea salt

2 Tbsp. parsley (fresh, chopped fine)

1 tsp. black pepper (fresh, ground)

2 Tbsp. oregano (chopped fine)

1 c. bread crumbs (whole wheat)

1 ½ lbs. turkey (ground, lean)

1 egg (beaten)

Directions:

1. Preheat the oven to 400 degrees. Line a baking pan with foil

2. Add the basil, garlic, salt, parsley, black pepper and oregano to a large-sized bowl. Mix in the bread crumbs, turkey and egg.

3. Use a rounded scoop to form the meatballs and set them on the baking pan. Set them in the oven to cook for about 20 minutes. Serve.

Italian Style Soup

Parmesan cheese, juicy turkey breasts, onions, spinach, and carrots make up this clean version of Italian soup.

Servings: 6

Ingredients:

¾ c. oat bran

1 lb. turkey (organic, ground, extra lean)

2 eggs (beaten)

3 Tbsp. onions (minced)

2 Tbsp. basil (fresh, minced)

3 Tbsp. parmesan cheese (grated, divided)

8 c. chicken broth (organic, low sodium)

2 c. spinach (rinsed, packed, chopped thin)

¾ c. carrots (diced)

Directions:

1. Mix together the oat bran, turkey, eggs, onions, basil, and 2 tablespoons of parmesan cheese. Use your hands to form small meatballs and place them aside for now.

2. Add the chicken broth, meatballs, spinach, and carrots to a large-sized pot. Set the heat to high and let it start to boil. Lower the heat down to medium.

3. Let the soup cook for about 10 minutes. Be sure the meatballs have completely cooked.

4. Sprinkle the remaining parmesan cheese on top before serving.

Zucchini Crisps

Zucchini is baked with sprinkles of parmesan cheese, cider vinegar, and homemade bread crumbs.

Servings: 2

Ingredients:

1/8 tsp. black pepper

¼ c. parmesan cheese (grated)

¼ c. bread crumbs (homemade from whole wheat bread)

1 c. milk (almond)

1 tsp. vinegar (apple cider)

½ c. flour (whole wheat)

2 ½ c. zucchini (sliced)

Directions:

1. Preheat the oven to 425 degrees.

2. Mix the black pepper, cheese, and bread crumbs in a medium-sized bowl.

3. Mix the milk, vinegar, and flour in a different bowl.

4. Take a slice of zucchini and dip it in the flour mix. Place it in the bread crumb mix next. Be sure it is coated well, and then place it on a baking pan. Repeat this process for the remaining zucchini slices.

6. Set the pan in the oven to bake for about 30 minutes. Be sure to flip the zucchini slices over after about 15 minutes.

Lemon Infused Tuna and Chickpea Salad

Roma tomatoes, onions, chickpeas, and tuna are mixed together in a delicious salad blend.

Servings: 12

Ingredients:

1 garlic clove (minced)

½ tsp. lemon zest

1 parsley bunch (flat leaf, chopped fine)

3 tomatoes (Roma, chopped)

Pepper (as desired)

1 Tbsp. olive oil

3 Tbsp. lemon juice

½ mint bunch (chopped fine)

½ onion (red, chopped fine)

2 16 oz. cans of chickpeas (rinsed, chopped roughly)

2 5 oz. cans of tuna (light, chunk, drained)

Directions:

1. Mix together the garlic, lemon zest, parsley, tomatoes, pepper, olive oil, lemon juice, mint, onions, and chickpeas using a large-sized bowl. Add the tuna and gently stir it in.

2. Serve.

Garlic and Rosemary Mashed Cauliflower

Greek yogurt is blended in with creamy cauliflower, garlic, rosemary, and delectable parmesan cheese.

Servings: 4

Ingredients:

1 cauliflower head (chopped)

¼ c. chicken stock (low sodium)

1 Tbsp. olive oil

1 Tbsp. yogurt (Greek, plain)

2 garlic cloves (chopped)

1 wedge of herb cheese

2 Tbsp. parmesan cheese (grated)

½ tsp. rosemary (fresh, chopped)

Sea salt (as desired)

¼ tsp. pepper

Directions:

1. Add the cauliflower to a large sized pot. Add enough water to cover the cauliflower then set the heat to medium-high. Let this boil for approximately 10 minutes. Drain the cauliflower thoroughly.

2. Pour the chicken stock into a food processor. Add the cauliflower, olive oil, yogurt, garlic and herb cheese, and parmesan cheese. Turn the processor on and let it process until everything is smooth.

3. Add the rosemary, salt, and pepper. Stir and serve.

Roma Tomato Guacamole

This guacamole dish is a blend of tomatoes, onions, garlic, avocados, and sprinkle of lime zest.

Servings: 8

Ingredients:

3 avocados (ripe, mashed lightly)

1 tsp. sea salt

2 limes (for juice)

Cilantro (fresh, chopped, as desired)

2 jalapenos (seeds removed, chopped)

1 garlic clove (minced)

2 tomatoes (Roma, chopped)

Cayenne pepper (as desired)

½ tsp. lime zest

½ onion (red, chopped)

Directions:

1. Mash up the avocados in a medium-sized bowl. Add the sea salt and lime juice continue mashing make sure everything is blended, but still chunky.

2. Add in the cilantro, jalapenos, garlic, tomatoes, cayenne, lime zest and onions. Mix well and serve.

Pecan and Nectarine Salad

This is a simple and quick lunch dish that mixes pecans, nectarines, and a sprinkle of spices.

Servings: 2

Ingredients:

2 nectarines (medium)

Allspice (as desired)

¼ c. pecans (raw, unsalted, chopped)

Directions:

1. Chop up the nectarines and take out the seeds.

2. Add the allspice, pecans and nectarines to a medium-sized bowl. Toss to coat everything.

3. Serve chilled.

Clean Coleslaw

Fresh green and red cabbages are tossed with garlic, onion, cider vinegar, and clean mayonnaise.

Servings: 6

Ingredients:

Pepper (as desired)

1 Tbsp. onion (chopped fine)

½ tsp. garlic powder

1 Tbsp. lemon juice

½ c. mayonnaise (organic)

1 c. red cabbage (shredded)

Sea salt (as desired)

½ tsp. celery seed

1 Tbsp. vinegar (apple cider)

2 c. green cabbage (shredded)

Directions:

1. Add the pepper, onion, garlic powder, lemon juice, mayonnaise, red cabbage, salt, celery seed, vinegar, and green cabbage to a large-sized bowl.

2. Make sure everything is blended well then place the bowl in the refrigerator to chill for about 2 hours.

3. Serve.

Orange and Asparagus Quinoa Salad

This salad blend mixes together fresh oranges, asparagus, pecans, dates, and delicious quinoa.

Servings: 8

Ingredients:

2 Tbsp. onions (red, minced)

1 c. quinoa (uncooked)

½ tsp. salt (Kosher)

2 c. water

¼ c. pecans (toasted, chopped)

1 c. oranges (fresh, sectioned)

½ jalapeno (diced)

5 dates (pits removed, chopped)

½ lb. asparagus (steam, chilled, sliced)

1 clove of garlic (minced)

2 Tbsp. lemon juice

¼ tsp. salt (Kosher)

1 Tbsp. olive oil (extra virgin)

¼ tsp. black pepper (fresh, ground)

2 Tbsp. mint (fresh, chopped)

Mint sprigs (as needed)

Directions:

1. Add the oil to a large-sized skillet. Set the heat to medium-high and add in the onions. Let them simmer for 2 minutes. Add the quinoa and continue cooking for about 5 minutes.

2. Pour in the salt and water. Cover the skillet and lower the heat to medium-low. Let this simmer for about 15 minutes. Take the pan away from heat and let it sit for approximately 15 minutes.

3. Move the mixture of quinoa to a large-sized bowl. Toss in the pecans, oranges, jalapeños, dates, and asparagus. Softly toss everything together.

4. For the dressing, mix together the garlic, lemon juice, salt, olive oil, and black pepper. Drizzle over the salad and then add in the chopped mint. Serve with sprigs of mint.

Honey and Rhubarb Salad

A mix of mango, green grapes, honey, rhubarb, and red grapes makes up this tasty fruit salad.

Servings: 8

Ingredients:

2 Tbsp. Grand Marnier

3 Tbsp. honey (raw, organic)

3 c. rhubarb (sliced thin)

1 ½ c. mango (diced)

1 ½ c. red grapes (cut in half)

1 ½ c. honeydew melon (chopped)

Directions:

1. Place the Grand Marnier, honey, and rhubarb in a medium-sized saucepan. Let it cook over medium heat for about 4 minutes. Be sure to stir a few times while it is cooking. Place in a large-sized bowl and let it chill in the refrigerator for approximately 15 minutes.

2. Add the mango, grapes and melon into the mixture of rhubarb. Stir gently then serve.

Celery and Scallion Salad

Crispy celery is sliced thin and served with fresh scallions drizzled in a blue cheese style dressing.

Servings: 6

Ingredients:

¼ tsp. salt

½ c. yogurt (plain, Greek, low fat)

½ c. buttermilk (organic)

½ tsp. hot sauce (organic)

¼ c. celery leaves (chopped)

½ c. and 2 Tbsp. scallions (sliced)

½ c. blue cheese (crumbled, divided)

3 c. celery (sliced)

Directions:

1. In a medium-sized bowl, whisk together the salt, yogurt, buttermilk, and hot sauce.

2. Add in the celery leaves, scallions (½ cup), blue cheese (¼ cup), and celery. Stir gently.

3. Serve with the remainder of the cheese and scallions as garnish.

Parmesan Smothered Broccoli

Fresh cooked broccoli is covered in a delicious parmesan cheese sauce with sprinkles of nutmeg and white pepper.

Servings: 4

Ingredients:

1 lb. broccoli

1 c. milk (nonfat, divided)

1 Tbsp. flour (almond)

¼ tsp. sea salt

½ c. parmesan cheese (fresh, grated)

Nutmeg (ground, as desired)

White pepper (as desired)

Directions:

1. Peel broccoli stems and cut into pieces. Break up florets into pieces. Add the broccoli to a large-sized pot and then pour in enough water to cover. Let it boil over medium-high heat. Let it boil for about 7 minutes or until desired texture.

2. In a small-sized bowl, whisk together the milk (1/4 cup) and flour.

3. Add the remainder of the milk to a medium-sized saucepan and warm it on medium-low. Add the flour mixture by whisking it in gradually for 4 minutes. Take away from the heat.

4. Add in the salt, cheese, nutmeg, and pepper. Stir. Pour over the broccoli and serve.

Red Bell Pepper Jambalaya with Quinoa

This version of jambalaya is blended using quinoa, garlic, red bell peppers, sausage, shrimp, and tomatoes.

Servings: 4

Ingredients:

2 chicken sausages (organic, sliced)

2 bell peppers (red, chopped)

2 garlic cloves (minced)

2 zucchinis (chopped)

½ c. quinoa (dry)

1 c. broth (chicken, organic)

1 28oz. can of tomatoes (diced)

½ lb. shrimp (peeled, veins removed)

Pepper (as desired)

Sea salt (as desired)

Directions:

1. Add the sausage, bell peppers, garlic, and zucchini to a large-sized pan and let them sauté for about 5 minutes on medium-high heat.

2. Stir in the quinoa and continue cooking for about 2 minutes. Pour in the broth and add the tomatoes. Let the mixture come to a boil then lower then heat to medium. Let it simmer for about 10 minutes.

3. Add in the shrimp and stir again. Cook for another 15 minutes.

4. Sprinkle in the pepper and sea salt. It's ready to serve.

Chicken Chili

This chili recipe uses fresh chicken, garlic, brown sugar, tomatoes, zucchini, and a spicy brown mustard.

Servings: 6

Ingredients:

1 Tbsp. garlic (minced)

2 lbs. chicken (organic, ground)

1 c. onions (chopped)

3 c. zucchini (chopped)

1 Tbsp. brown sugar (raw, organic)

2 tsp. cumin

3 15oz. cans of tomatoes (diced)

2 Tbsp. mustard (spicy, organic)

1 Tbsp. chili powder

1 tsp. salt

4 Tbsp. vinegar (apple cider)

1 Tbsp. mustard (yellow, organic)

Directions:

1. In a large-sized pot, add the garlic, chicken, and onions. Let them cook over medium-high heat until they have browned. Break up the ground chicken while it cooks. Add the mixture to the crock pot.

2. Add in the zucchini, brown sugar, cumin, tomatoes, spicy mustard, chili powder, salt, vinegar, and yellow mustard. Stir to mix all ingredients well.

3. Set the crock pot on low and cook for about 2 hours. Serve.

Bananas with Honey Cinnamon Glaze

Bananas are cooked in a delicious honey sauce with cinnamon added to the mix.

Servings: 2

Ingredients:

2 tsp. honey (raw, organic)

½ tsp. cinnamon

1 banana (large, sliced)

Directions:

1. Mix the honey and cinnamon in a small-sized bowl.

2. Coat a non-stick pan with olive oil cooking spray. Set the pan over medium heat and add in the slices of banana.

3. Cook for about 1 ½ minutes on each side. Pour the honey mixture on top of the banana slices and flip them over to coat the mixture evenly.

4. Cook for just about 10 seconds on each side and serve.

Chive and Rosemary Spread over Whole Wheat

This recipe is a mix of rosemary, chives, lemon juice, cashews, and delicious garlic.

Servings: 7

Ingredients:

1 c. cashews (raw)

1 Tbsp. water

1 garlic clove (large)

1 Tbsp. lemon juice (fresh)

1 Tbsp. chives (chopped)

1 tsp. rosemary (chopped)

1 tsp. yeast seasoning (organic)

¼ tsp. salt

½ tsp. onion powder

7 slices of bread (whole wheat)

Directions:

1. In a medium-sized pot, add the cashews and enough water to cover them. Let them boil on medium-high heat, and then lower it down to medium. Let this cook for approximately 20 minutes.

2. Take the cashews out and place them in the food processor. Let them process for about 3 minutes. Add in 1 tablespoon of water then the garlic, lemon juice, chives, rosemary, yeast seasoning, salt and onion powder.

3. Pulse gradually so that everything is well blended. Place in an air-tight container to chill for a few hours. Serve on top of whole wheat bread.

Apple Pear and Walnut Salad

Pears, apples, walnuts, grapes, thyme, are blended with agave nectar for this fresh salad dish.

Servings: 4

Ingredients:

1 apple (medium, diced)

1 pear (Barlett, diced)

2 tsp. lemon juice (fresh)

1 tsp. thyme leaves (fresh, chopped)

1 c. grapes (red, sliced in half)

¼ c. pomegranate seeds

Cinnamon (ground, as desired)

¼ c. walnuts (cut in half)

Agave nectar (raw, organic, as desired)

Directions:

1. In a medium-sized bowl, add the apples and pears. Pour in the lemon juice and toss to coat the fruit thoroughly.

2. Add in the thyme, grapes, and pomegranate. Stir. Toss in the cinnamon and walnuts. Toss one more time. Pour the agave nectar over the salad and serve.

Spinach Shrimp and Mushroom Salad

Fresh shrimp, crimini mushrooms, thyme, spinach, chives, and avocados make up this tasty salad.

Servings: 2

Ingredients:

1/8 tsp. sea salt

3 tsp. olive oil

1/8 tsp. black pepper (fresh, ground)

1 8oz. pack of mushrooms (crimini, cut into quarters)

4 sprigs of thyme (chopped)

1 tsp. seasoning salt (all-purpose, salt free)

½ lb. shrimp (peeled, deveined, remove the tails)

2 tsp. chives (chopped)

2 tsp. lemon juice (fresh)

1 ½ Tbsp. olive oil (extra virgin)

¼ c. farro (cooked)

4 c. spinach (baby)

½ avocado (sliced)

Directions:

1. Add the oil (2 teaspoons) to a large-sized pan. Toss in the salt, pepper, mushrooms, and thyme. Let this simmer for approximately 8 minutes.

2. Lower the heat and take out the mushrooms. Put them somewhere to stay warm. Set the heat to medium and add more oil (1 teaspoon). Toss in the seasoning salt and shrimp. Let the shrimp cook for about 3 minutes on each side or until cooked.

3. To mix the salad, add the chives, lemon juice, olive oil, farro, and spinach to a large-sized bowl. Toss and then divide the salad up into 2 separate bowls. Add some avocado, shrimp and mushrooms to each bowl.

4. Serve.

Pine Nuts Tomato Basil Salad

Crunchy pine nuts are mixed together with tomatoes, garlic, sea salt, basil and sprinkled with olive oil

Servings: 2

Ingredients:

2 tomatoes (large)

Sea salt (as desired)

2 garlic cloves (peeled, chopped)

1/3 c. basil (packed loose, chopped)

½ c. pine nuts (raw)

Olive oil (extra virgin)

Directions:

1. Chop up the tomatoes. Set them on a serving platter.

2. Add the salt, garlic, basil, and pine nuts to a food processor. Let this process until a crumb texture is formed.

3. Sprinkle on a little bit of the olive oil on top of the tomatoes. Add the pine nut mixture on top.

4. Serve.

Peach Cucumber Gazpacho

This gazpacho recipe blends together shallots, cucumbers, peaches, lemon juice, and bell peppers.

Servings: 6

Ingredients:

1 cucumber (large, peeled, chopped)

¼ c. shallots (chopped)

2 Tbsp. lemon juice (fresh)

1 c. water

1 c. walnuts (raw)

2 c. peaches (peeled, chopped)

1 bell pepper (yellow, chopped)

1 c. basil (fresh)

Sea salt (as desired)

Directions:

1. Add the cucumbers, shallots, lemon juice, water, walnuts, peaches, bell pepper, basil and sea salt to a blender.

2. Turn on the highest blending speed and let it process until the texture becomes completely smooth. Place in an airtight container and let it chill for a few hours before serving.

Black Bean Peach Salad

Fresh peaches are tossed together with avocados, cilantro, onions, bell peppers, and wholesome black beans.

Servings: 4

Ingredients:

1 jalapeno (remove the seeds, diced)

1 bell pepper (red, chopped fine)

¼ onion (red, diced fine)

2 peaches (firm, organic, chopped fine)

1 16 oz. can of black beans (drained, rinsed)

½ c. cilantro (fresh, chopped fine)

Sea salt (as desired)

½ tsp. cumin

1 avocado (firm, chopped)

2 Tbsp. lime juice

2 tsp. olive oil (extra virgin)

Directions:

1. Add the jalapeno, bell pepper, onion, and peaches to a large-sized glass bowl. Mix gently.

2. Add in the black beans and cilantro. Stir again and then add the salt and cumin. Toss lightly and softly add the avocado in and drizzle the lime juice and olive oil on top. Toss again.

3. Chill for a few minutes then serve.

Clean Eating Cookbook

Vol.3

Dinner Recipes

Mango Salsa Salmon

This salmon recipe is a blend of garlic, oregano, cumin, cayenne, mangos, and fresh cilantro.

Servings: 2

Ingredients:

½ c. cilantro (fresh, minced)

¼ c. onion (red, peeled, diced)

1 tomato (medium, seeds removed, chopped)

1 mango (ripe, peeled, pitted, chopped)

1 Tbsp. lime juice (fresh)

1 clove of garlic (peeled, crushed)

1 tsp. oregano (dried, ground)

1/8 tsp. cayenne pepper

¼ tsp. white pepper (fresh, ground)

1 tsp. cumin (ground)

1 Tbsp. paprika

¼ tsp. black pepper (fresh, ground)

½ tsp. garlic powder (salt-free)

2 8oz. salmon filets (wild caught)

2 Tbsp. olive oil (extra virgin)

Directions:

1. In a small-sized bowl, mix together the cilantro, onion, tomato, mango, lime juice, and garlic. Cover the bowl and let the salsa refrigerate for now.

2. Use a separate small-sized bowl and mix together the oregano, cayenne, white pepper, cumin, paprika, black pepper, and garlic powder. Dry the salmon using paper towels. Lightly press the salmon into the spice bowl, making sure each piece is evenly coated.

3. Add the oil to skillet (cast iron) and set the heat to high. Set the salmon in the pan and let it cook for about 2 minutes on each side until it is fully cooked. Serve with mango salsa.

Bison Chili

The flavors of bison, tomatoes, sweet onions, red beans, and chili powder are blended together in this chili recipe.

Servings: 6

Ingredients:

1 onion (large, sweet, diced)

4 Tbsp. chili powder

1 lb. bison meat (ground, grass-fed)

1 Tbsp. cumin

3 cans of red beans (organic, drained and rinsed)

2 c. chicken broth (organic, low sodium)

2 tomatoes (large, cut into cubes)

Directions:

1. In a large-sized pot, add the onion, chili powder, bison, and cumin. Let this cook over medium heat until the bison has browned completely. Crumble meat as it cooks.

2. Add in the red beans, broth and tomatoes. Let it start to boil then cover the pot. Leave the lid slightly off. Lower the temperature to low and continue simmering for about 2 hours. Stir occasionally.

Crispy Almond Mahi Mahi

Savory mahi mahi is covered in delicious almonds, black pepper, and sea salt, with a hint of fresh lemon juice.

Servings: 4

Ingredients:

4 Mahi mahi fillets (wild caught)

1 Tbsp. oil (coconut, melted)

½ tsp. sea salt

1 tsp. black pepper

½ c. almond meal

1 tsp. thyme

1 lemon (for juice)

Directions:

1. Preheat the oven to 350 degrees.

2. Set the filets in a glass baking dish and add the coconut oil on top of the filets.

3. Mix together the sea salt, black pepper, almond meal, and thyme in a small-sized bowl. Take the mixture and dust it on top of the filets. Drizzle the lemon juice on next.

4. Set the filets in the oven and let them cook for about 25 minutes or until fully cooked.

5. Serve.

Cranberry Lettuce Wraps with Turkey

Fresh cranberries, green onions, juicy turkey, and crispy lettuce leaves are all a part of this dinner dish.

Servings: 8

Ingredients:

1 Tbsp. olive oil (extra virgin)

1 tsp. cumin

1/3 c. cranberries (dried)

2 c. turkey (cooked, chopped, organic)

1 apple (core removed, chopped)

3 onions (green, sliced)

Black pepper (as desired)

Sea salt (as desired)

8 lettuce leaves (large, organic)

1 16oz. can of cranberry sauce (whole, organic)

Directions:

1. Preheat the oven to 350 degrees.

2. Warm the olive oil on medium heat, in a large-sized skillet. Add in the cumin, cranberries, turkey, apple, and onions. Let this mixture cook, while stirring for a few minutes. Be sure the apples are cooked through and then add in the pepper and salt.

3. Divide the mixture up and distribute it on the lettuce leaves. Tuck the sides of the lettuce in and roll them up.

4. Add the cranberry sauce to the bottom of a glass baking dish. Spread it out evenly and then set the lettuce rolls on it with the seams facing down.

5. Cover the dish with aluminum foil and place the dish in the oven to cook for about 20 minutes.

6. Take the dish out of the oven and let it cool for a few minutes before serving.

Eggplant and Basil Pasta

Eggplant is cooked alongside creamy pasta, cherry tomatoes, garlic, and onions.

Servings: 6

Ingredients:

2 garlic cloves (minced)

1 eggplant (medium)

2 Tbsp. olive oil (extra virgin)

¼ c. onions (chopped)

2 c. tomatoes (chopped)

¼ c. basil (chopped)

1 c. cherry tomatoes (sliced in half)

1/8 tsp. black pepper

¼ tsp. sea salt

2 Tbsp. pine nuts

¼ c. parmesan cheese (grated)

6 oz. penne pasta (whole wheat)

Directions:

1. Cook pasta according to package instructions. Drain pasta and set aside. In a large-sized skillet, add the garlic, eggplant, oil, and onions. Let this cook over medium-high heat until the onions have softened.

2. Add in the chopped tomatoes and let it start to boil. Lower the heat to medium-low and continue cooking for about 5 minutes.

3. Add in the basil, cherry tomatoes, pepper, and salt. Cook for a few more minutes.

4. Add the pasta to a large sized serving bowl and pour the tomato mixture in with it. Toss gently to coat and sprinkle on the pine nuts and parmesan cheese.

Roasted Eggplant and Tomatoes

Eggplant is mixed with tomato sauce, red pepper, capers, and savory garlic.

Servings: 4

Ingredients:

4 eggplants (small, organic)

1 lb. penne pasta (whole grain)

Sea salt (as needed)

3 c. tomato sauce (organic)

Red pepper flakes (as needed)

½ c. basil (fresh, chopped)

¼ c. capers (rinsed, chopped coarsely)

6 garlic cloves (minced)

Black pepper (fresh, ground, as desired)

2 Tbsp. olive oil (extra virgin)

Directions:

1. Preheat the oven to 450 degrees. Use a fork to poke holes all over the eggplant. Set the eggplant on a flat baking pan and place it in the oven to cook for approximately 40 minutes.

2. Take the eggplant out of the oven and let it cool for about 10 minutes. Once cool, peel and take out the seeds and pulp. Chop the pulp up and drain the juices from it.

3. Add the pasta to a large-sized pot and pour in enough water to cover. Sprinkle a little bit of sea salt in and stir. Cook to el dente stage.

4. In a large-sized skillet, add the tomato sauce and set the heat to medium. Let it warm a little, then add in the eggplant, red pepper flakes, basil, capers, garlic, black pepper, and olive oil.

5. Drain the pasta and place it on serving plate. Add the eggplant mixture on top and serve.

Cilantro Lime Shrimp

Fresh shrimp is cooked with paprika, curry powder, and cayenne pepper, serve garnished with lime and cilantro.

Servings: 4

Ingredients:

1/8 tsp. cinnamon

½ tsp. curry powder

1 tsp. paprika

1/8 tsp. cayenne pepper

½ tsp. cumin (ground)

¾ tsp. sea salt

2 lbs. shrimp (large, peeled, deveined)

Butter (grass-fed, as desired)

Cilantro (fresh, chopped, as desired)

Lime wedges (as needed)

Directions:

1. Mix the cinnamon, curry powder, paprika, cayenne, cumin, and salt in a small-sized bowl. Add the shrimp to a large-sized bowl and sprinkle the spice mixture on top. Toss the shrimp to coat evenly.

2. Add the butter to a large-sized pan and set the heat to medium-high. Let the butter melt and then add in the shrimp. Cook while stirring for

approximately 5 minutes or until shrimp are cooked through. Sprinkle cilantro and lime juice on top.

Garlic Chicken Bruschetta

Juicy chicken breasts are cooked along with garlic, onions, tomatoes, basil, and sea salt.

Servings: 4

Ingredients:

Black pepper (as desired)

1/8 tsp. sea salt

4 chicken breasts (organic)

Basil (fresh, chopped)

1 tsp. vinegar (balsamic)

½ onion (red, small, chopped)

4 tomatoes (small, chopped)

1 tsp. olive oil (extra virgin)

1 garlic clove (minced)

Directions:

1. Preheat the oven to 375 degrees.

2. Sprinkle the pepper and salt on top of the chicken breasts and place them in a glass dish. Cover the dish with foil and place it in the oven to cook for approximately 40 minutes.

3. In a large-sized bowl, add the basil, vinegar, onion, chopped tomatoes, olive oil and garlic. Mix well and place in the refrigerator while the chicken is still cooking.

4. Once the chicken is done, place each piece on a serving plate and top with the tomato mixture. Serve.

Garlic Thyme Lemon Chicken

Fresh thyme, lemon, garlic, and sea salt are cooked with tasty chicken breasts.

Servings: 4

Ingredients:

1 tsp. pepper

1 Tbsp. thyme (fresh)

1 lemon (for zest)

½ tsp. sea salt

2 garlic cloves (minced)

2 lemons (for juice)

4 chicken breasts (organic)

Directions:

1. Preheat the oven to 375 degrees.

2. In a small-sized bowl, mix together the pepper, thyme, lemon zest, salt, garlic, and lemon juice using a whisk.

3. Set the chicken in a glass baking pan and drizzle the lemon mixture on top. Be sure that the chicken is completely coated.

4. Set the pan in the oven and let the chicken back for about 40 minutes or until done.

Green and Clean Pasta Salad

Asparagus, garlic, honey, onions, chicken breasts, and creamy yogurt are mixed together for this dish.

Servings: 8

Ingredients:

Sea salt (as desired)

2 c. asparagus (chopped)

Cooking spray (olive oil)

1 garlic clove (minced)

1 Tbsp. lemon juice (fresh)

½ c. yogurt (Greek, plain)

1 Tbsp. honey (raw)

¼ c. coconut milk (light)

Black pepper (as desired)

¼ c. dill (fresh)

¼ c. parsley (fresh, flat leaf)

12 oz. penne pasta (whole wheat)

¼ c. mint (fresh)

¼ c. cilantro (fresh)

12 oz. chicken breasts (skinless, boneless, cooked, chopped, organic)

3 onions (green, sliced)

Directions:

1. Add water to a large-sized pot and sprinkle a little bit of salt in it. Let the water boil over medium-high heat.

2. Add in the asparagus and let it cook for about 1 minute. Take the asparagus out and immediately put in cold water. Drain and place in a large-sized bowl.

3. Cook pasta according to package instructions. While the cooked pasta is draining, spray it with cooking spray and toss just a little.

4. To make the dressing, add the garlic, lemon juice, yogurt, honey, and coconut milk to a small-sized bowl. Whisk to blend everything completely. Sprinkle in some pepper and salt and whisk again.

5. Add the onions, dill, parsley, pasta, mint, cilantro, chicken, and asparagus to a large-sized bowl. Toss and then pour in the dressing. Toss again. Sprinkle with more pepper and salt. Garnish with green onions.

6. Serve.

Cucumber Sauce Smothered Crab Cakes

Crispy lettuce, chives, cucumber, yogurt, crab, and fresh lemon make up this delectable dinner recipe.

Servings: 4

Ingredients:

½ cucumber (peeled, cut in half, seeds removed)

12 chives (fresh, sliced)

2/3 c. yogurt (plain, reduced fat)

Black pepper (fresh, ground, as desired)

Sea salt (as desired)

1 1/3 c. panko bread crumbs (whole wheat)

1 Tbsp. lemon juice

½ c. bell pepper (red, seeds removed, chopped)

1 lb. crab meat (lumped, cooked)

1 lemon (for zest)

5 egg whites (large)

2 Tbsp. sunflower oil

8 lettuce leaves (butter, large)

Directions:

1. Add the cucumber, chives, and yogurt to the food processor. Sprinkle in the pepper and salt. Blend until the mixture has a pureed texture.

2. Mix together salt, panko, lemon juice, bell pepper, crab, and lemon zest in a large-sized bowl. Add in the egg whites. Use your hands to mix everything completely and start forming the mixture into rounded cakes. Place them on a baking pan when finished.

3. Place 2 medium-sized skillets on medium heat. Add oil to both. Place 4 cakes in each skillet. Let them cook for approximately 4 minutes on each side.

4. Separate the lettuce and place a lettuce leaf on each serving plate. Split the cakes up among the plates and add a couple of tablespoons of the cucumber sauce to each plate. Use the remainder of the sauce as garnish for serving.

Cucumber Mint Grilled Fish

Fresh mint and cucumbers are combined with grilled cod and crispy green onions.

Servings: 4

Ingredients:

Olive oil (extra virgin)

¼ tsp. black pepper (fresh, ground)

1 Tbsp. sea salt

½ tsp. oregano (dried)

4 5oz. cod filets (wild caught)

3 Tbsp. cucumber (English, chopped fine)

½ onion (green, chopped fine)

1 Tbsp. mint leaves (fresh, chopped fine)

¼ c. yogurt (Greek, plain)

Directions:

1. Add the oil to a large-sized pan and set it over high heat.

2. Use the pepper, ¼ teaspoon of salt, and the oregano to sprinkle over both sides of the filets. Place them in the pan.

3. Let them cook for about 3 minutes on each side until done.

4. In a small-sized bowl, mix together the cucumber, onion, mint, yogurt and the remainder of the salt. Put some of this cucumber mixture on top of each filet.

Lemon and Garlic Tuna Burgers

These tuna patties are a mix of onions, parsley, dill, eggs, and fresh lemon juice.

Servings: 12

Ingredients:

1 tsp. garlic powder

1 tsp. parsley (dried)

2 Tbsp. lemon juice (fresh)

3 eggs (organic, cage free)

½ tsp. dill (dried)

½ c. onion (red, chopped)

3 5oz. cans of tuna (packed in water, no salt, drained)

Olive oil (extra virgin, as needed)

Directions:

1. Add the garlic powder, parsley, lemon juice, eggs, dill, onion, and tuna to a medium-sized bowl. Mix together thoroughly.

2. Use your hands to roll the mixture and then flatten it out into patties.

3. Add oil to the pan and set it over medium-high heat. Cook the patties in batches for a few minutes on each side.

Stuffed Sweet Potato (Mexican Style)

A mix of black beans, avocado, cheddar cheese, and yogurt are blended and stuffed into creamy sweet potatoes.

Servings: 1

Ingredients:

1 sweet potato (organic, medium)

1 tsp. lime juice (fresh)

2 Tbsp. yogurt (Greek, plan, nonfat)

1/3 c. corn and black bean salsa (organic)

¼ c. cheddar cheese

¼ avocado (diced)

Directions:

1. Use a fork to poke holes all over the sweet potato.

2. Set the sweet potato on a plate that is microwavable. Place it in the microwave and let it cook for about 8 minutes on the highest power. Take the potato out and let it cool for just a few minutes.

3. Slice the sweet potato in half and use a fork to fluff up the inside. Mix together the lime juice and yogurt in a small sized bowl. Add the salsa on top of the potato and follow with the cheese and avocado. Place the yogurt mixture on top and serve!

Zucchini Pesto Quinoa

Zucchini and quinoa are blended together with basil pesto and parmesan cheese.

Servings: 7

Ingredients:

4 c. zucchini (raw, grated)

¼ c. parmesan cheese (grated)

4 c. quinoa (cooked)

½ c. pesto (basil, organic)

Directions:

1. Add the zucchini, cheese, quinoa, and pesto to a large-sized bowl. Stir until everything is well blended.

2. Serve at room temperature, warmed, or chilled.

Baby Spinach Pear Sandwich

Savory baby spinach is cooked with a hint of lemon juice and mixed with pears over whole grain bread.

Servings: 4

Ingredients:

1 tsp. lemon juice (fresh,)

2 tsp. oil (canola)

2 pears (large, Bosc, core and seeds removed, chopped)

4 slices of bread (whole grain)

1 c. baby spinach (cooked)

Directions:

1. Preheat the oven to 400 degrees.

2. In a medium-sized bowl, add the lemon juice and canola oil. Mix together thoroughly.

3. Add the pears to the bowl and mix to make sure they are coated evenly.

4. Set the pears on a baking pan and place them in the oven to cook for about 20 minutes. They should be golden when they are ready.

5. Take the bread and toast it just a little. Place on serving plates when it is done. Add some pears on next and then some spinach. Place another slice of toast on top.

Cucumber Mozzarella Quinoa Salad

This quinoa salad blends flavors of tomatoes, cucumbers, mozzarella, broccoli, carrots, ginger, and garlic.

Servings:

Ingredients:

1 can of beans (garbanzo, drained)

1 cucumber (chopped0

5 basil leaves (large, fresh, sliced)

1 lemon (for juice)

1 c. broccoli sprouts

Black pepper (as desired)

Vinegar (balsamic, as desired)

Sea salt (as desired)

Olive oil (extra virgin, as desired)

1 c. mozzarella cheese (low fat, chopped)

2 carrots (baby, diced)

1 tsp. ginger root (grated)

2 garlic cloves (medium, diced)

1 tomato (chopped)

1 c. quinoa (cooked)

Directions:

1. In a large-sized bowl, mix together the beans, cucumber, basil, lemon juice, broccoli sprouts, pepper, vinegar, salt, oil, cheese, carrots, ginger, garlic, tomatoes, and quinoa.

2. Toss to be sure everything is coated well then place in the refrigerator for approximately 30 minutes.

3. Take the bowl out, toss again and serve.

Herb Seasoned Arugula Linguine

A mix of parmesan cheese, arugula, garlic, basil, tomatoes, red pepper flakes, parsley, and thyme make up this recipe.

Servings: 8

Ingredients:

¼ c. olive oil (extra virgin)

2 garlic cloves (minced)

2 c. arugula (baby, fresh)

1 13oz. pack of linguine (whole wheat)

1 Tbsp. capers (drained, diced)

2 c. grape tomatoes (cut in half)

1 Tbsp. basil (fresh, chopped)

¼ tsp. pepper flakes (red, crushed)

1 Tbsp. parsley (fresh, chopped)

½ tsp. black pepper

2 thyme sprigs (remove the stems)

Sea salt (as desired)

¼ c. parmesan cheese (fresh, grated)

Directions:

1. Cook pasta according to package instructions and then drain. Add the oil to a large-sized pan and set the heat on medium-low. Let it warm then toss in the garlic and cook for about 1 minute.

2. Add in the arugula and pasta. Stir. Add in the capers, basil, red pepper flakes, parsley, black pepper, thyme, and sea salt. Stir as it cooks. Once the arugula has gone limp, take it away from the heat and toss in the tomatoes. Stir softly to mix.

3. Add the cheese on top and serve.

Turkey Sausage and Green Onion Jambalaya

Juicy turkey, green onions, brown rice, and green bell peppers make this jambalaya recipe.

Servings: 4

Ingredients:

1 green pepper (chopped)

8 oz. turkey sausage (sliced)

Sea salt (as desired)

8 oz. chicken tenders (sliced)

1 15oz. can of tomatoes (stewed)

1 c. brown rice (instant, organic)

½ c. water

1 bunch of onions (green, sliced)

Directions:

1. Warm a large-sized pan over medium heat. Add in the green pepper and sausage and let it cook for about 5 minutes while stirring.

2. Add the salt, chicken, tomatoes (with the juice), water, and rice. Let the mixture start to boil then set the heat down to low. Cover the pan and let the mixture simmer for about 10 minutes or until chicken is cooked.

3. Take the pan away from the heat and toss in the green onions. Stir and serve.

Garlic Lime Turkey Soup

Turkey mixes with lime, garlic, corn, thyme, squash, and bell peppers in this delectable dinner.

Servings: 6

Ingredients:

2 tsp. canola oil

1 bell pepper (red, cored and seeds removed, chopped)

2 leeks (trimmed, chopped)

3 garlic cloves (chopped fined)

2 Tbsp. thyme (fresh, chopped)

4 c. chicken broth (organic, low sodium)

1 ½ tsp. cumin (ground)

1 ½ lbs. butternut squash (peeled, seeded, chopped into cubes)

2 c. corn (frozen)

1 lb. turkey cutlets (organic, sliced into strips)

½ tsp. red pepper (crushed)

2 Tbsp. lime juice (fresh)

Black pepper (as desired)

Sea salt (as desired)

Directions:

1. Add the oil to a large-sized pot. Set the heat to medium and let the oil warm. Add in the bell pepper and leeks. Stir and let it cook for about 4 minutes. Add in the garlic and continue cooking for about 1 minute.

2. Add the thyme, broth, cumin, and squash. Stir and let it start to boil. Set the heat on medium-low. Continue cooking for approximately 10 minutes.

3. Toss in the corn and turkey. Let it simmer for about 4 minutes or until turkey is cooked. Pour in the crushed red pepper and then the lime juice. Let the soup continue to simmer on low for 4 minutes. Sprinkle with pepper and salt before serving.

Thai Style Lime Ginger Chicken

This is a quick and simple dinner recipe that blends flavors of garlic, ginger, lime, peanuts, and savory chicken.

Servings: 2

Ingredients:

1/3 c. peanuts (dry roasted, no salt)

1 ½ tsp. ginger (ground)

1 ½ Tbsp. garlic powder

½ lb. chicken breasts (skinless, boneless, organic)

1 lime (for juice)

Directions:

1. Preheat the oven to 375 degrees.

2. Place the peanuts in a small food processor and let them process until they are a fine grained texture. Pour them into a small-sized bowl.

3. Add in the ginger and garlic powder and stir.

4. Set the chicken on a flat baking pan and drizzle the lime juice on top. Make sure it completely coats the chicken. Take each piece of chicken and roll it around in the peanut mixture then put it back on the baking pan.

5. Set the pan in the oven and let the chicken bake for about 25 minutes or until done.

6. Serve.

Balsamic Glazed Chicken Bites

Garlic, balsamic vinegar, honey, and parsley and blended over crispy chicken tenders.

Servings: 4

Ingredients:

Cooking spray (olive oil, as needed)

12 oz. of chicken tenders (organic)

Black pepper (as desired)

Sea salt (as desired)

1 tsp. garlic (minced)

¼ c. chicken broth (organic, low sodium)

1 Tbsp. honey (raw)

3 Tbsp. vinegar (balsamic)

Parsley (fresh)

Directions:

1. Coat a pan with cooking spray and set it on medium-high heat. Add the chicken tenders. Sprinkle the pepper and salt on top. Cook the chicken for about 3 ½ minutes on each side or until cooked through. Take the chicken out of the pan and set it aside to keep warm.

2. Lower the heat to medium-low and add in the garlic. Let it simmer for a few minutes before adding the broth, honey, and vinegar. Continue to let this simmer for about 1 minute while scraping the pan.

3. Add the chicken back into the pan and stir the mixture. Let everything warm through completely then sprinkle fresh parsley on top. Serve immediately.

Pumpkin Plum Tomato Pasta

Whole wheat spaghetti is mixed with delicious cream cheese, red pepper, pumpkin, turkey, and tomatoes.

Servings: 6

Ingredients:

1 onion (chopped)

1 lb. turkey (ground, lean, organic)

1 clove of garlic

1 zucchini (chopped0

1 tomato (plum, chopped)

1 carrot (shredded)

10 oz. spaghetti sauce (organic)

13 oz. spaghetti (whole wheat)

1 15oz. can of pumpkin (organic)

1 red pepper (roasted)

1 Tbsp. cream cheese (reduced fat)

Directions:

1. Cook pasta according to package instructions and drain. Add the onions, turkey and garlic to a large-sized skillet. Cook the mixture over medium-high heat. Crumble the turkey as it cooks until it has browned completely.

2. Add in the zucchini, tomato, and carrots. Let this simmer for about 5 minutes. Toss in the pasta sauce, pasta, pumpkin, and red pepper. Continue to let this simmer for about 10 minutes.

3. Add the cream cheese in next and immediately take the skillet away from the heat. Let the cream cheese melt on its own and then stir it into the sauce.

4. Let the mixture cool for a few minutes. Serve.

Olive Tomato Tilapia

White wine is cooked into fresh tilapia, garlic, tomatoes, and pepper.

Servings: 4

Ingredients:

¼ tsp. black pepper (fresh, ground)

¼ tsp. sea salt

2 Tbsp. olive oil (extra virgin)

1 ¼ lbs. tilapia

3 garlic cloves (chopped)

¼ c. white wine (dry)

1 c. cherry tomatoes (sliced in half)

3 Tbsp. tapenade (olive)

Directions:

1. Dust the pepper and salt on top of the tilapia. Add the oil (1 tablespoon) to a large-sized skillet. Set the heat to medium-high and let it warm.

2. Add the fish to the skillet and let it cook for about 6 minutes or until done, flipping it over after 3 minutes. Place the fish on a large-enough serving plate. Lightly cover with foil to keep fish warm.

3. Add the remainder of the oil to the pan. Add in the garlic, wine, and tomatoes. Set the heat to medium and cook for about 5 minutes, stirring occasionally.

4. Add the olive tapenade in and continue cooking for about 1 minute. Serve the sauce with the fish.

Beef Smothered Delicata Squash

A mix of beef, onions, yogurt, and chili powder are stuffed into soft delicata squash.

Servings: 4

Ingredients:

6 tsp. olive oil (extra virgin, divided)

2 Delicata squash (small, cut in half and seeded)

½ tsp. sea salt (divided)

1 c. water

½ c. bulgur

1 onion (small, chopped)

2 Tbsp. chili powder

8 oz. beef (lean, ground, grass-fed)

½ c. yogurt (plain, nonfat)

4 tsp. shelled pumpkin seeds (toasted)

Directions:

1. Preheat the oven to 425 degrees.

2. Spread the oil (2 teaspoons) on the squash sides that are cut. Sprinkle on part of the salt (1/4 teaspoon). Set the squash on a baking pan, making sure the cut sides are facing down. Place in the oven to cook for about 30 minutes.

3. In a small-sized saucepan, add the water and bulgur. Let it boil over medium-high heat, then lower the heat to medium-low. Cook for approximately 10 minutes. Drain.

4. In a large-sized skillet, warm the rest of the oil on medium heat. Add in the onions and let them simmer for about 5 minutes. Add the chili powder, beef and the remainder of the salt. Stir while it cooks for approximately 5 minutes or until beef is browned.

5. Add the bulgur in with the beef and then pour in the yogurt.

6. Stir the mixture well and then scoop approximately ¾ cup of the mixture out and place it in each squash. Sprinkle pumpkin seeds on each and serve.

Thai Style Sautéed Mussels

Fresh mussels are seasoned and simmered in lime juice, brown sugar, basil, fish sauce, garlic, and green curry.

Servings: 4

Ingredients:

1 Tbsp. olive oil (extra virgin)

2 cloves of garlic (minced)

1 Tbsp. fish sauce (Thai)

2 tsp. curry paste (green, Thai)

14 oz. coconut milk (lite)

1 Tbsp. brown sugar (organic)

2 Tbsp. lime juice (fresh)

4 lbs. mussels (cleaned)

½ c. cilantro (fresh)

½ c. basil (fresh)

Directions:

1. Add the oil to a large-sized pot. Set the heat on medium. Toss in the garlic and let it simmer for approximately 1 minute.

2. Add the fish sauce, curry paste, milk, brown sugar, and lime juice. Set the heat to high and let it start to boil. Add the mussels in and cover the pot. Let this cook for about 6 minutes or until mussels are opened. Throw away any unopened mussels.

3. Take the pot away from the heat and then add in the cilantro and basil. Use the sauce in the pan as garnish for serving.

Shrimp and Cod Tomato Mix

This mix features flavors of Alaskan cod, fresh shrimp, oregano, garlic, and juicy tomatoes.

Servings: 6

Ingredients:

2 Tbsp. olive oil (extra virgin)

6 garlic cloves (minced)

5 tomatoes (large, chopped)

1 ½ Tbsp. oregano (dried)

½ lb. shrimp (large, peeled, deveined)

1 lb. cod (Alaskan)

Sea salt (as desired)

Directions:

1. Add the olive oil to a large-sized skillet and set the heat to medium-high. Add the garlic and let it cook until it is browned.

2. Add in the tomatoes and stir. Add some of the oregano (1 teaspoon) to the mixture and stir again.

3. Set the shrimp and cod on top of the tomato mixture and sprinkle the salt on. Cover the skillet and let it simmer for about 3 minutes. Take the top off, flip the fish over and sprinkle with salt again and the remaining oregano. Cover and continue cooking for about 3 minutes or until fish is cooked.

4. Take the cover off and turn off the heat. Leave the skillet in place and let it sit for about 3 minutes. Serve.

Sweet and Spicy Salmon

Salmon is glazed and cooked with garlic, cinnamon, apricot nectar, honey, soy sauce, and ginger.

Servings: 4

Ingredients:

1/3 c. apricots (dried, chopped)

2 Tbsp. soy sauce (organic, low sodium)

2 garlic cloves (minced)

1/8 tsp. cayenne pepper

¼ tsp. cinnamon (ground)

1 Tbsp. ginger (fresh, grated)

2 Tbsp. honey (organic)

1 ½ c. apricot nectar

1 ¾lb. salmon fillet (skin removed)

Directions:

1. Turn the broiler on.

2. Grease a pan for broiling.

3. Mix the dried apricots, soy sauce, garlic, cayenne, cinnamon, ginger, honey, and apricot nectar in a medium-sized saucepan. Set the heat on medium and let it start to boil. Set the heat on medium-low and continue cooking for approximately 20 minutes. Take out some of the glaze (1/4 cup), and set the rest aside.

4. Set the salmon on the pan and use a brush to add the glaze to each filet. Place the pan in the oven and let the filet broil for about 6 minutes before flipping the filets over and add a little more glaze. Continue cooking for another 6 minutes.

5. Serve the salmon with the remainder of the glaze.

Italian Basil Flounder

This flounder recipe mixes together garlic powder, tomatoes, juicy flounder, basil, and a hint of lemon.

Servings: 4

Ingredients:

4 2lbs. flounder (filets)

½ Tbsp. butter (grass-fed)

Black pepper (fresh, as desired)

Sea salt (as desired)

1 Tbsp. lemon juice

1 tsp. garlic powder

½ c. tomato (fresh, diced)

2 tsp. basil (dried)

Directions:

1. Preheat the oven to 350 degrees.

2. Place the flounders in a medium-sized glass baking dish. Add a little bit of butter to each and then sprinkle on the pepper and salt. Add a little more salt over all the filets and pour the lemon juice on top of that.

3. Add the garlic powder, tomato, and basil on next. Cover the dish and place it in the oven to bake for about 30 minutes.

4. Take the dish out and serve.

Garlic Clam Sauce with Spaghetti

A mix of garlic, onions, spaghetti, tomatoes, baby clams, and fresh parsley make up this pasta dish.

Servings: 4

Ingredients:

2 Tbsp. olive oil (extra virgin)

1 c. onions (minced)

4 tsp. garlic (minced)

¼ tsp. black pepper (fresh, ground)

¼ tsp. sea salt

1 15oz. can of tomatoes (organic, diced, drained)

1 Tbsp. lemon juice (fresh)

2/3 c. white wine (dry)

2 10oz. cans of clams (baby, drained)

8 oz. spaghetti (whole wheat, cooked)

Directions:

1. Add the oil to a large-sized skillet. Let it warm on medium heat, then toss in the onions. Let them simmer for about 4 minutes.

2. Add in the garlic and let it simmer for about 1 minute. Toss in the pepper, salt, and tomatoes. Continue cooking for about 3 minutes.

3. Pour the lemon juice and wine in. Set the heat to low and continue cooking for about 3 minutes.

4. Add the clams and pasta. Stir to blend everything together. Serve.

Garlic Carrot Pasta

Carrots, garlic, and fresh thyme make up the majority of this delicious dish.

Servings: 2

Ingredients:

4 carrots (large, peeled)

Olive oil (extra virgin, as needed)

5 thyme sprigs (leaves removed, discard stems)

6 cloves of garlic (minced)

1 c. chicken broth (organic)

Black pepper (fresh, as needed)

Sea salt (as needed)

Directions:

1. Use a spiralizer to slice the carrots. Set this aside for now.

2. A little bit of olive oil to a large-sized skillet and set the heat to medium. Toss in half of the thyme sprigs and the garlic. Stir while letting it simmer for approximately 10 minutes.

3. Stir while pouring in the chicken broth and then add the carrots in. Let this cook until the carrots are slightly limp, but still firm. Sprinkle the pepper and salt.

4. Serve with the remainder of the thyme sprigs.

Black Bean Quinoa with Tomatoes

Delicious quinoa is served with savory black beans, oregano, cracked pepper, kale, and tomatoes.

Servings: 2

Ingredients:

1 c. quinoa (cooked)

2 c. black beans (organic, cooked)

½ tsp. oregano (dried)

1 tsp. chili powder

1 tsp. cumin

4 kale leaves (trimmed, chopped)

5 tomatoes (medium, cut into quarters)

Black pepper (fresh, cracked, as desired)

Sea salt (as desired)

Directions:

1. In a large-sized pan, add the cooked quinoa and beans. Set the heat on medium-low and add in the oregano, chili powder, and cumin. Stir.

2. Add in the kale and tomatoes. Stir and let it cook long enough for the kale to go limp.

3. Sprinkle on the pepper and salt. Serve.

Turkey Vegetable Mix Meatloaf

Onions, garlic, sage, carrots, eggs, turkey, rosemary, and cracked pepper are blended together for one healthy meal.

Servings: 4

Ingredients:

1 egg (organic, cage free)

¼ c. carrots (diced)

2 garlic cloves (minced)

1 Tbsp. rosemary (fresh, chopped)

½ tsp. sea salt

¼ c. ketchup (organic)

2 lbs. turkey (organic, ground)

¼ c. green pepper (diced)

¼ c. onions (diced)

2 Tbsp. Worcestershire sauce

1 Tbsp. sage (fresh, chopped)

½ tsp. black pepper (fresh, cracked)

2 slices of toast (whole wheat, toasted, made into crumbs)

Directions:

1. Preheat the oven to 350 degrees.

2. In a large-sized bowl, mix together the egg, carrots, garlic, rosemary, salt, ketchup, turkey, green pepper, onions, Worcestershire sauce, sage, black pepper, and toast crumbs.

3. Make sure the mixture is well combined. Use your hands to mix it a little more. Place the mixture in an appropriately sized loaf pan. Pat it down to make it even then place it in the oven to bake for about 1 hour and 15 minutes.

4. Take it from the oven and let it sit for about 5 minutes. Remove from pan and slice to serve.

Black Bean and Tomato Chicken

Savory chicken is mixed together with black beans, corn, chilies, and juicy tomatoes.

Servings: 4

Ingredients:

1 15oz. can of tomatoes (diced, organic)

4 chicken breasts (organic, skinless, boneless)

1 Tbsp. chili powder

1 ¼ c. corn (frozen, organic)

1 16oz. can of black beans

1 can of chilies (small, diced)

¼ c. green onions (sliced)

Avocado (as needed)

Cilantro (as needed)

Lime (fresh, as needed)

Directions:

1. In a large-sized skillet, add the tomatoes, chicken, and chili powder. Set the heat on medium-high and let this cook for about 30 minutes or until chicken is cooked, stirring occasionally.

2. Add in the corn, beans, and chilies. Sprinkle the pepper and salt in. Continue cooking for about 7 minutes.

3. Add the green onions in and stir. Serve with avocado, cilantro, and lime on top.

Blood Orange Dungeness Crab

Fresh Dungeness crab is mixed with garlic, shallots, red pepper, parsley, thyme, and fresh blood orange peel.

Servings: 2

Ingredients:

½ c. butter (grass-fed)

¼ c. olive oil (extra virgin)

1 ½ tsp. red pepper (dried, crushed)

1 Tbsp. shallot (minced)

2 Tbsp. garlic (minced)

2 Tbsp. parsley (fresh, chopped)

2 Tbsp. thyme (fresh, chopped)

2 Dungeness crabs (large, cooked, cleaned, cracked)

1 tsp. blood orange grated peel

½ c. juice from blood orange

Directions:

1. Preheat the oven to 500 degrees.

2. In a large skillet that is oven-safe, add the butter and oil. Set the heat to medium-high and let it melt before stirring in the red pepper, shallot, and garlic. Add the crabs.

3. Take half of the parsley and thyme and sprinkle it over the crabs. Stir everything so that it is blended well. Set the skillet in the oven and let it bake for about 12 minutes or until crab is cooked.

4. Take the skillet out and move the crabs to a serving plate.

5. Add the orange peel and orange juice to the skillet the crab was just in. Place it back on medium-high heat and let about half of the sauce cook out. Spoon this sauce mixture over the crabs and add the remainder of the parsley and thyme. Serve immediately.

Mango and Sesame Chicken

Sesame seeds, ginger, lime, garlic, savory chicken breasts and delicious mango make up this dinner dish.

Servings: 4

Ingredients:

Rice (organic, cooked)

2 ½ c. water

2 Tbsp. sesame seeds

1 tsp. olive oil (extra virgin)

¼ tsp. ginger

4 garlic cloves (minced)

¼ tsp. black pepper (fresh, ground)

1 lb. chicken breasts (organic, skinless, boneless)

1 mango (peeled, diced)

½ lime (for juice)

3 tomatoes (medium, organic, chopped)

Directions:

1. Mix water, rice and salsa in a pan. Cook rice according to package instructions.

2. Add the sesame seeds to a small-sized pan and let them toast for about 3 minutes on low heat.

3. In a large-sized pan, add the oil. Let it warm on low heat and then add the ginger, garlic, black pepper, and chicken. Turn the heat up to medium cook for approximately 4 minutes on each side or until chicken is cooked.

4. Add the mango directly on top of the chicken. Stir while cooking for approximately 2 minutes. Add in the lime juice and tomatoes. Stir and let this simmer for about 5 minutes.

5. Add the sesame seeds in, stir again, and serve with the rice.

Jerked Tilapia

Tilapia is cooked in a number of flavors like garlic, cinnamon, jalapeno, cloves, sea salt, and thyme to give it that jerk seasoning flavor.

Servings: 2

Ingredients:

½ tsp. chili powder

½ tsp. ginger

¼ tsp. cinnamon

½ tsp. thyme

1 Tbsp. garlic (minced)

½ of a jalapeno pepper (core and seeds removed, chopped fine)

½ tsp. black pepper

Sea salt (as desired)

1/8 tsp. cloves (ground)

½ Tbsp. lime juice

¼ tsp. nutmeg

2 5oz. tilapia filets (wild caught)

1 Tbsp. olive oil (extra virgin)

Directions:

1. In a small-sized bowl, mix the chili powder, ginger, cinnamon, thyme, garlic, jalapeno, black pepper, salt, cloves, lime juice, and nutmeg.

2. Place the filets in a large sized bowl and add the olive oil. Coat both sides of the filets and then sprinkle on the spices. Make sure the spices coat both sides.

3. Add a little bit of oil to a large-sized skillet. Cook the filets, over medium heat, for approximately 3 minutes for each side or until done. Serve immediately.

Conclusion

Thank you again for taking the time to look through my clean eating recipes. I personally believe that the food we eat has a huge impact on our long-term health and more studies are confirming it every day. With a focus on whole and natural foods, you are protecting your health for the long term. People have even claimed to have clearer skin, lose weight and better digestion after switching to a clean eating lifestyle.

As always I recommend checking out numerous clean eating recipe books so you have a nice variety of recipes and avoid getting bored with what you eat.

Happy eating!

Charity Wilson

.

Clean Eating Smoothies

Healthy Recipes Supporting A Whole Foods Lifestyle

Strawberry Green Granola Smoothie

Servings: 1

Ingredients:

1 tsp. granola clusters

3/4 c. fresh organic strawberries

1/2 c. crushed ice cubes

1 c. raw spinach

1 tsp. honey

Directions:

Put all ingredients in a blender and blend until smooth.

Nutritional Info Per Serving:

Calories 71, Carbs 17 g, Fat 1 g, Protein 2 g

Clean Blueberry Cheese Smoothie

Servings: 1

Ingredients:

1 c. almond milk

1 c. kale

½ c. crushed ice cubes

1/2 c. low-fat cottage cheese

1/2 c. frozen organic blueberries

Directions:

Put all ingredients in a blender and blend until smooth.

Nutritional Info Per Serving:

Calories 248, Carbs 32 g, Fat 5 g, Protein 19 g

Clean Banana Butter Smoothie

Servings: 1

Ingredients:

1 banana

1/2 c. crushed ice cubes

1 c. almond milk

1 tsp. flaxseeds

1 tsp natural peanut butter

Directions:

Put all ingredients in a blender and blend until smooth.

Nutritional Info Per Serving:

Calories 211, Carbs 37 g, Fat 6 g, Protein 4 g

Cranberries-Pecan Swirl Smoothie

Servings: 1

Ingredients:

1/2 c. cranberries, sliced

1 c. almond milk

1 tsp. cinnamon

1/2 c. chopped pecans

1/2 c. crushed ice

1 tsp. honey

Directions:

Put all ingredients in a blender and blend until smooth.

Nutritional Info Per Serving:

Calories 457, Carbs 29 g, Fat 38 g, Protein 7 g

Raspberry Coffee Smoothie

Servings: 1

Ingredients:

1 tbsp. roasted coffee beans

1 c. almond milk

1 c. frozen raspberries

1/2 c. crushed ice

Directions:

Put all ingredients in a blender and blend until smooth.

Nutritional Info Per Serving:

Calories 321, Carbs 74 g, Fat 3 g, Protein 3 g

Almond-Quinoa Smoothie

Servings: 1

Ingredients:

1 tbsp. chopped almonds

1 c. coconut milk

1/2 c. crushed ice

1/4 c. cooked quinoa

Directions:

Put all ingredients in a blender and blend until smooth.

Nutritional Info Per Serving:

Calories 642, Carbs 24 g, Fat 51 g, Protein 9 g

Green Berry & Nut Smoothie

Servings: 1

Ingredients:

¼ c. strawberries

1 c. almond milk

¼ c. blueberries

¼ c. collard greens

¼ c. chopped pecans

¼ c. chopped walnuts

1/2 c. crushed ice

Directions:

Put all ingredients in a blender and blend until smooth.

Nutritional Info Per Serving:

Calories 484, Carbs 24 g, Fat 41 g, Protein 12 g

Green Blueberry Tea Smoothie

Servings: 1

Ingredients:

1 c. almond milk

1 c. green tea

1/4 c. blueberries

1/2 c. crushed ice

Directions:

Put all ingredients in a blender and blend until smooth.

Nutritional Info Per Serving:

Calories 81, Carbs 13 g, Fat 3 g, Protein 1 g

Pear Oatmeal Smoothie

Servings: 1

Ingredients:

1 c. dry oatmeal

1 c. sliced pears

1 c. almond milk

1 tsp. honey

1/2 c. crushed ice

Directions:

Put all ingredients in a blender and blend until smooth.

Nutritional Info Per Serving:

Calories 484, Carbs 94 g, Fat 8 g, Protein 12 g

Cinnamon Strawberry Yogurt Smoothie

Servings: 1

Ingredients:

1/4 c. Greek yogurt

1 c. strawberries

1 tbsp. cinnamon

1 c. coconut milk

1/2 c. crushed ice

Directions:

Put all ingredients in a blender and blend until smooth

Nutritional Info Per Serving:

Calories 648, Carbs 32 g, Fat 58 g, Protein 13 g

Pecan Berry Smoothie

Servings: 1

Ingredients:

1/4 c. chopped pecan nuts

1/2 c. frozen blueberries

1 c. almond milk

1 tsp. honey

1/2 c. crushed ice

Directions:

Put all ingredients in a blender and blend until smooth.

Nutritional Info Per Serving:

Calories 318, Carbs 28 g, Fat 23 g, Protein 5 g

Raspberry Swirl Smoothie

Servings: 1

Ingredients:

1 tbsp. flaxseed oil

1/4 c. frozen raspberries

1/2 tsp. cinnamon

1 c. almond milk

1 tsp. honey

1/2 c. crushed ice

Directions:

Put all ingredients in a blender and blend until smooth.

Nutritional Info Per Serving:

Calories 279, Carbs 31 g, Fat 17 g, Protein 2 g

Apricot Chocolate Smoothie

Servings: 1

Ingredients:

1/4 c. apricot

1 c. almond milk

1 tsp. flaxseeds

1 c. low-fat chocolate milk

1/2 c. crushed ice

Directions:

Put all ingredients in a blender and blend until smooth.

Nutritional Info Per Serving:

Calories 251, Carbs 39 g, Fat 6 g, Protein 10 g

Green Tangerine Yogurt Smoothie

Servings: 1

Ingredients:

1 c. Greek yogurt

1/4 c. tangerine

1 c. raw spinach

1 c. almond milk

1/2 c. crushed ice

Directions:

Put all ingredients in a blender and blend until smooth.

Nutritional Info Per Serving:

Calories 223, Carbs 24 g, Fat 3 g, Protein 26 g

Ginger Berry Smoothie

Servings: 1

Ingredients:

¼ c. frozen blueberries

¼ c. frozen raspberries

1 tsp. ginger

1/2 c. crushed ice

1 c. almond milk

Directions:

Put all ingredients in a blender and blend until smooth.

Nutritional Info Per Serving:

Calories 151, Carbs 31 g, Fat 3 g, Protein 2 g

Strawberry Spice Smoothie

Servings: 1

Ingredients:

1 tsp. ginger

1 tsp. ground cloves

1 tsp. cinnamon

1 tsp. strawberries

1 c. almond milk

1 tsp. honey

1/2 c. crushed ice

Directions:

Put all ingredients in a blender and blend until smooth.

Nutritional Info Per Serving:

Calories 101, Carbs 18 g, Fat 3 g, Protein 1 g

Peach Walnut Pie Smoothie

Servings: 1

Ingredients:

½ peach, peeled

1 tbsp. fat-free whip cream

1 tbsp. chopped walnuts

1 c. almond milk

1 tsp. honey

1/2 c. crushed ice

Directions:

Put all ingredients in a blender and blend until smooth.

Nutritional Info Per Serving:

Calories 151, Carbs 20 g, Fat 7 g, Protein 3 g

Spicy Raspberry Smoothie

Servings: 1

Ingredients:

1 c. raspberries

1 tsp. cinnamon

1 tsp. ginger

1 tsp. cayenne

1 c. almond milk

1/2 c. crushed ice

Directions:

Put all ingredients in a blender and blend until smooth.

Nutritional Info Per Serving:

Calories 142, Carbs 27 g, Fat 4 g, Protein 3 g

Peach Tea Smoothie

Servings: 1

1 c. almond milk

1 peach, sliced

1 c. green tea

1/2 c. crushed ice

Directions:

Put all ingredients in a blender and blend until smooth.

Nutritional Info Per Serving:

Calories 98, Carbs 17 g, Fat 3 g, Protein 2 g

Green Apple Smoothie

Servings: 1

Ingredients:

1 c. kale

1 Honey Crisp apple, sliced

1 c. almond milk

1/2 c. crushed ice

Directions:

Put all ingredients in a blender and blend until smooth.

Nutritional Info Per Serving:

Calories 172, Carbs 37 g, Fat 3 g, Protein 3 g

Honey Nut Cheerios Smoothie

Servings: 1

Ingredients:

1 tbsp. honey

1/4 c. cashews

¼ c. almonds

1 c. almond milk

1/2 c. crushed ice

Directions:

Put all ingredients in a blender and blend until smooth.

Nutritional Info Per Serving:

Calories 458, Carbs 42 g, Fat 30 g, Protein 11 g

Green Banana Walnut Smoothie

Servings: 2

Ingredients:

1 c. coconut milk

1/4 c. walnuts

1 banana, sliced

1 c. raw spinach

1/2 c. crushed ice

Directions:

Put all ingredients in a blender and blend until smooth.

Nutritional Info Per Serving:

Calories 429, Carbs 22 g, Fat 38 g, Protein 8 g

Cinnamon Green Watermelon Smoothie

Servings: 1

Ingredients:

1 cup 1-inch cubes seeded watermelon

1 tbsp. cinnamon

1 c. almond milk

1 c. kale

1/2 c. crushed ice

Directions:

Put all ingredients in a blender and blend until smooth.

Nutritional Info Per Serving:

Calories 145, Carbs 30 g, Fat 3 g, Protein 4 g

Minty Strawberry Smoothie

Servings: 1

Ingredients:

1 c. strawberry

1 tsp. mint leaves

1 c. almond milk

1 c. kale

1/2 c. crushed ice

Directions:

Put all ingredients in a blender and blend until smooth.

Nutritional Info Per Serving:

Calories 140, Carbs 26 g, Fat 3 g, Protein 4 g

Syrupy Pineapple Smoothie

Servings: 1

Ingredients:

1 c. pineapples

1/4 c. sugar-free maple syrup

1 c. almond milk

1/2 c. crushed ice

Directions:

Put all ingredients in a blender and blend until smooth.

Nutritional Info Per Serving:

Calories 235, Carbs 53 g, Fat 3 g, Protein 1 g

Honeydew Cream Smoothie

Servings: 1

Ingredients:

1 cup 1-inch cubes honeydew

1 tsp. cinnamon

2 tbsp. fat-free whip cream

1 c. almond milk

1/2 c. crushed ice

Directions:

Put all ingredients in a blender and blend until smooth.

Nutritional Info Per Serving:

Calories 131, Carbs 27 g, Fat 3 g, Protein 1 g

Banana Nut Spice Smoothie

Servings: 1

Ingredients:

1 banana, sliced

1 tbsp. pecans

½ tsp ginger

½ tsp nutmeg

1 c. almond milk

1/2 c. crushed ice

Directions:

Put all ingredients in a blender and blend until smooth.

Nutritional Info Per Serving:

Calories 272, Carbs 38 g, Fat 13 g, Protein 4 g

Spicy Cantaloupe Tea Smoothie

Servings: 1

Ingredients:

1 c. green tea

1 tsp. cayenne

1 c. cantaloupe, sliced

1 c. coconut milk

1/2 c. crushed ice

Directions:

Put all ingredients in a blender and blend until smooth.

Nutritional Info Per Serving:

Calories 611, Carbs 27 g, Fat 58 g, Protein 7 g

Ginger Peach Smoothie

Servings: 1

Ingredients:

1 peach, peeled

1 tbsp. ginger

1 tsp. flaxseed oil

1 c. coconut milk

1/2 c. crushed ice

Directions:

Put all ingredients in a blender and blend until smooth.

Nutritional Info Per Serving:

Calories 652, Carbs 27 g, Fat 63 g, Protein 7 g

Sweet Spinach Raspberry Smoothie

Servings: 1

Ingredients:

1 c. raspberries

1 c. raw spinach

1 tbsp. cinnamon

1 c. coconut milk

1/2 c. crushed ice

Directions:

Put all ingredients in a blender and blend until smooth.

Nutritional Info Per Serving:

Calories 640, Carbs 35 g, Fat 58 g, Protein 8 g

Blue and Green Carrot Smoothie

Servings: 1

Ingredients:

¼.c. blueberries

1 carrot, sliced

1 c. almond milk

1 c. kale

1/2 c. crushed ice

Directions:

Put all ingredients in a blender and blend until smooth.

Nutritional Info Per Serving:

Calories 157, Carbs 31 g, Fat 3 g, Protein 4 g

Pear Cream Smoothie

Servings: 1

Ingredients:

1/4 c. Greek yogurt

1 tbsp. fat-free whip cream

1/2 c. pear

1 c. almond milk

1/2 c. crushed ice

Directions:

Put all ingredients in a blender and blend until smooth.

Nutritional Info Per Serving:

Calories 142, Carbs 23 g, Fat 3 g, Protein 7 g

Green Honeydew Smoothie

Servings: 1

Ingredients:

1 lime, sliced

1 c. honeydew, sliced

1 c. almond milk

1 c. kale

1/2 c. crushed ice

Directions:

Put all ingredients in a blender and blend until smooth.

Nutritional Info Per Serving:

Calories 174, Carbs 38 g, Fat 3 g, Protein 4 g

Cinnamon Green Apple Smoothie

Servings: 1

Ingredients:

1 tbsp. cinnamon

1 green apple, sliced

1 c. almond milk

1 tsp. honey

1/2 c. crushed ice

Directions:

Put all ingredients in a blender and blend until smooth.

Nutritional Info Per Serving:

Calories 193, Carbs 44 g, Fat 3 g, Protein 1 g

Vanilla Blueberry Smoothie

Servings: 1

Ingredients:

1 tbsp. vanilla extract

1 c. frozen blueberries

1 c. coconut milk

1/2 c. crushed ice

Directions:

Put all ingredients in a blender and blend until smooth.

Nutritional Info Per Serving:

Calories 672, Carbs 36 g, Fat 58 g, Protein 7 g

Hot Raspberry Smoothie

Servings: 1

Ingredients:

1 c. frozen raspberries

1 tsp. cayenne

1 c. almond milk

1 tsp. honey

1/2 c. crushed ice

Directions:

Put all ingredients in a blender and blend until smooth.

Nutritional Info Per Serving:

Calories 345, Carbs 80 g, Fat 3 g, Protein 3 g

Blueberry Carrot-Cucumber Smoothie

Servings: 1

Ingredients:

1 cucumber, sliced

1 carrot

1/2 c. frozen blueberries

1 c. almond milk

1/2 c. crushed ice

Directions:

Put all ingredients in a blender and blend until smooth.

Nutritional Info Per Serving:

Calories 172, Carbs 35 g, Fat 3 g, Protein 4 g

Conclusion

I hope you found some new and exciting smoothies inside. They will compliment any lifestyle and beat sugary drinks any day. When you are first transitioning to a clean eating lifestyle take it slow.

If you try eliminating all the junk in one day chances are you will end up just binging. Instead look to gradually eliminate the excess processed foods from your diet and you will eventually just not eat them anymore.

I hope you embrace a clean eating lifestyle and protect your health. There are other diets with fancy names like anti-inflammatory, Mediterranean, etc. but they are all close to being the same with one focus: eating whole, raw foods for health.

I hope you enjoy the recipes.

Charity Wilson

Charity Wilson

About The Author

Charity Wilson is the loving mother of four children, well five if you count her husband of over 25 years. She has worked in various jobs over the years but realized one day home is where she needed to be. After a lot of deliberation and research, she decided to become a full-time writer.

Being a full time at home mom and writer sounds like a lot of work and for good reason, it is. She loves every minute of the organized chaos that is her daily life. It is what fuels her ideas and inspires her to write the books she does. She loves to share what she knows and is always willing to learn something new.

She loves to cook and create new recipes which you will find shared throughout her various cookbooks. She stays up to date on the most current diets but doesn't particularly follow any one of them. She eats to enjoy while consciously watching her health. She knows people need a variety of recipes to avoid the boredom that leads to weight gain and tries to fill that void.

Her passions don't stop at cooking and she is an avid gardener, organizer and loves reading. She is known amongst the kids in the sports community as "the lady with the best chocolate chip cookies ever." She enjoys being able to watch her children play sports and is quite active herself. In the end, you could call her a homebody.

Charity is all about living life with passion and enjoying every moment. Life is about enjoying good food, great company and waking up every day happy to do it all over again.

http://www.amazon.com/Charity-Wilson/e/B00JOMC93G/

Charity Wilson

Copyright/Disclaimer

The information provided in this book is for educational and entertainment purposes only. The author is not a physician and this is not to be taken as medical advice or a recommendation to stop taking medications. The information provided in this book is based on the author's experiences and interpretations of the past and current research available. You should consult your physician to insure the daily habits and principles in this book are appropriate for your individual circumstances. If you have any health issues or pre-existing conditions, please consult your doctor before implementing any of the information you have learned in this book. Results will vary from individual to individual. This book is for informational purposes only and the author does not accept any responsibilities for any liabilities or damages, real or perceived, resulting from the use of this information.

Respective authors own all copyrights not held by the publisher.

The information herein is offered for informational purposes solely, and is universal as so. The presentation of the information is without contract or any type of guarantee assurance.

The trademarks that are used are without any consent, and the publication of the trademark is without permission or backing by the trademark owner. All trademarks and brands within this book are for clarifying purposes only and are owned by the owners themselves, not affiliated with this document.

Made in the USA
Middletown, DE
11 October 2016